*Uncle John's*

## Plunges Into

# NEW YORK

PORTABLE
PRESS

Ashland, Oregon

# Uncle John's
## Plunges Into
# NEW YORK

The Bathroom Readers' Institute would like to thank the following people whose advice and assistance made this book possible:

| | |
|---|---|
| Gordon Javna | Dan Mansfield |
| JoAnn Padgett | Jenness Crawford |
| Melinda Allman | Ryan Murphy |
| J. Carroll | Terri Schlichenmeyer |
| Lorraine Bodger | Beth Fhaner |
| Sue Steiner | Leslie Elman |
| Derek Fairbridge | Peter Norton |
| Stephanie Spadaccini | Sean Moore |
| Emma Borghesi | John Hogan |
| Carl Lavo | Jay Newman |
| Thom Little | Blake Mitchum |
| Brian Boone | Aaron Guzman |

Cover design by Rusty von Dyl and Emma Borghesi
Interior layout and design by Moseley Road

For information, write:
The Bathroom Readers' Institute, P.O. Box 1117, Ashland, OR 97520
www.bathroomreader.com ★ e-mail: mail@bathroomreader.com

ISBN-13: 978-1-62686-044-5

Library of Congress Cataloging-in-Publication Data

Uncle John's plunges into New York.
    pages cm
    ISBN 978-1-62686-044-5 (hardcover)
1.  New York (N.Y.)--Miscellanea. 2.  New York (N.Y.)--Anecdotes. 3.
New York (N.Y.)--Humor. 4.  Curiosities and wonders--New York
(State)--New York.  I. Bathroom Readers' Institute (Ashland, Or.) II.
Title: Plunges into New York.
    F128.36.U53 2014
    974.7'1--dc23
                                2013043008

Printed in Huizhou, China
First Printing
1 2 3 4 5    19 18 17 16 15

# Contents

# Start Spreadin' the News!

## Welcome to the Concrete Jungle

The editors of the Bathroom Readers' Institute have outdone themselves with this special (let's call it "irregular") illustrated edition all about the world's most fabulous city—New York!

No other city is as impressive as the Big Apple. The sheer size of it! The excitement! The entertainment! Millions of people—from first-time visitors to lifelong natives—have been mesmerized by the dizzying array of high-rises, the bright lights, the nonstop action, the celebrities… and the traffic jams. The Big Apple really does have it all, and so does this book, complete with dazzling photos that bring the stories to life!

Like every edition of *Uncle John's Bathroom Reader*, this volume is a treasure trove of the most offbeat and hilarious topics, fascinating facts, little-known history, and astounding mysteries—plus trivia, quotes, and really strange stuff about the city that never sleeps. So settle back with an Italian ice, and dig into the best of New York:

**Origins.** The rise of skyscrapers, Central Park, the Apollo Theater, and the New York Public Library (where, according to the rules, you must wear clothes).

**People.** Have you heard about swindlers who actually "sold" the Brooklyn Bridge? Can you spot a hipster in a crowd of New Yorkers? And what's with the guy who plays guitar in Times Square, wearing only a cowboy hat, boots, and his underwear?

**Mystery and Intrigue.** Delve into the New York City murder case that inspired Edgar Allan Poe, witness the birth of the New York Mafia, and ponder what's down in the sewers (*lots* of things, actually).

**Go Outside!** Escape city life with a visit to a park on top of a Manhattan wastewater treatment plant, stalk the famous hawk that nests on Fifth Avenue, and marvel at the city's celestial event—Manhattanhenge.

**Yum!** Sample New York's culinary delights, from foods as ubiquitous as bagels, soft pretzels, and Reuben sandwiches to rare delicacies like Nesselrode pie.

**Eww!** Try not to touch anything as you uncover the city's dirtiest problems, including sewage overflows, trash pileups, dog poop, and bedbugs.

**Strange, but True.** Gasp in disbelief at New York's wildest weather, weirdest news, looniest laws, and wackiest hoaxes—including the 140-year-old hot dog at Coney Island and newspaper accounts of life on the Moon.

**Note:** It turns out there's a whole state out there called New York. Travel to odd pit stops, view strange statues, explore heart-stoppingly beautiful parks, and learn about the day Niagara Falls was "turned off."

But before you go, we want to give a big New York shout-out to every member of the talented team that contributed to this book, all of whom deserve a knish, a hot dog with everything, and a supersized egg cream. And now you get to reap the benefits of their hard work. Happy reading!

And as always…

*Go with the flow!*

**—Uncle John and the BRI staff**

*Facing page: New York City and the Hudson River*

# Hole in One

*In more than 100 years of bagel making, New Yorkers have acquired such a passion for the doughy bread that it has become an internationally known icon of the city. But the bagel isn't actually a native New Yorker.*

*New York bagel*

## Bagel Tales

There's a lot of debate over how bagels came to be. One story says a 17th-century Austrian baker wanted to make a gift for King John III Sobieski of Poland, who saved Austria from a Turkish invasion. The king was a famous horseman, so the baker shaped the dough like a stirrup. (The Austrian word for "stirrup" is *bügel*.)

Another story goes like this: Around 1610 the first bagel, called a *beygl* in Yiddish, came out of a Jewish oven in Krakow, Poland. Historians say the doughnut-shaped rolls were designed to be gifts for Jewish women with infants—the hole in the bread represented the gift of life and the crusty roll was a useful teething ring. Also, unlike other breads, bagels could be boiled before the Jewish Sabbath, left until after the religious observance 24 hours later (Jewish law forbade cooking on the Sabbath), and then quickly baked to perfection. People loved them.

No matter where they came from, bagels invaded the United States in the late 19th century by way of Jewish immigrants from eastern Europe. Vendors typically sold them as street food, but by 1907, one group of prominent New York bagel makers had founded the International Bagel Bakers Union to protect their recipes. Not just anyone could join; only the sons of former members were eligible. The union's leader, Moishe Soprano, was tough and no-nonsense—he secured contracts with nearly all the bakeries in the New York City area, ensuring bagel-making consistency for decades. A union contract also gave the consumers peace of mind—Soprano and his bakers kneaded their dough by hand, unlike "lower-end" bagel makers outside the union who, rumor had it, often kneaded the dough with their feet.

## Bagels for All

After World War I, Canadian bagel maker Meyer Mickey Thompson tried to create an automated bagel maker. He failed

*Tower of Bagel*

because his invention was too expensive, but his son Daniel succeeded in creating the Thompson Bagel Machine, and started churning them out in the 1960s in a six-car garage in New Haven, Connecticut. Thompson Bagel Machines could produce about 400 bagels an hour at minimal cost. Bagel bakers Harry Lender and Florence Sender took it from there, using the machines to mass-produce frozen bagels and selling them to supermarkets everywhere.

In 1988 Americans ate an average of one bagel a month. Five years later, it was a bagel every two weeks and growing.

## Bagel Bits

- In North America, there are two types of bagels: The New York version and the Montreal. The New York contains salt and malt, and is boiled in water and then baked so that it's puffy with a moist crust. The Montreal is smaller due to a larger hole, and has no salt. It's

*Tax collectors shuttered H&H Bagels in Manhattan for three hours in 2009 until the owner paid his back taxes.*

# Big Bagel

According to *Guinness World Records*, the world's largest bagel was made by Bruegger's in Syracuse, New York.

**Weight:** 868 pounds.
**Diameter:** 6 feet.
**Thickness:** 20 inches.

*Montreal bagel*

boiled in honey-sweetened water and then baked in a wood-fired oven, making it crunchy and sweet.

- To New York's chagrin, the first bagel in space was the Montreal version. In 2008 Canadian-born astronaut Gregory Chamitoff lifted off in the space shuttle *Discovery* with a shipment of 18 sesame-seed bagels from his cousin's bakery in Montreal and delivered them to the International Space Station.

- In the spring of 2009, New York State tax

collectors shut down H&H Bagels in Manhattan (popularized on the TV show *Seinfeld*) for failing to pay $100,000 in back taxes. For three hours, customers stood forlorn outside the closed bagel emporium until owner Helmer Toro came up with a $25,000 payment that allowed H&H to reopen.

*Gregory Chamitoff introduced bagels to outer space.*

9

# The Swingingest Borough

*New Orleans is often cited as the birthplace of jazz, and Chicago, Harlem, and Kansas City are recognized as critical launching pads for the music. But the borough of Queens is where the coolest cats chose to crash when they were beat, ya dig?*

*Louis Armstrong plays the blues.*

## What a Wonderful Neighborhood

In 1943, after more than two decades of traveling and performing, jazz great Louis "Satchmo" Armstrong and his wife, Lucille, settled down for the first time and bought a house at 34-56 107th Street in Corona, Queens. It remained his home until his death in 1971, and after Lucille passed away in 1983, the two-story house became the Louis Armstrong House Museum. To this day, the interiors are preserved as the Armstrongs left them, and the den features an extensive archive of Satchmo's personal reel-to-reel recordings. And although Armstrong mostly maintained a level of modesty appropriate for a man who grew up in the New Orleans Home for Colored Waifs, he did allow himself certain household indulgences,

including a kitchen with all its appliances built in (including the blender) and gold trumpetlike faucets in the bathroom.

Why did Satchmo settle in Queens? The cultural diversity and domestic possibilities that Queens offered are best summed up by Armstrong himself: "I am here with the black people, with the Puerto Rican people, the Italian people, the Hebrew cats, and there's food in the Frigidaire. What else could I want?" He wasn't the only jazz great to call Queens home.

## The Saints of St. Albans

Many notable musicians made their homes in the Queens neighborhood of St. Albans, particularly in the enclave of Addisleigh Park. A list of the notable residents reads like a poster for a jazz festival:

*Trumpetlike fixtures give the golden bathroom of the Louis Armstrong House Museum extra flair.*

- **Fats Waller** (173–19 Sayres Avenue): This master "tickler" (jazz slang for "piano player") and writer of such classics as "Ain't Misbehavin'" and "Honeysuckle Rose" came to the neighborhood in 1938. Many jazz historians name him as the first African American to call Addisleigh Park home. His house boasted a Steinway grand piano and a built-in Hammond organ.

- **Count Basie** (174–27 Adelaide Road): A native of Red Bank, New Jersey, Basie and his wife, Catherine, lived in Addisleigh Park from 1946 to 1971. The Basies were popular among neighborhood youths for generously granting access to their backyard pool.

- **Ella Fitzgerald** (179–07 Murdock Avenue): The "First Lady of Song" never had a stable home as a child. Her parents separated when she was young, her mother died when she was a teenager, her stepfather abused her—and there were stopovers at reform school, a period of homelessness, and a short stint working as a lookout at a New York bordello. But as a teenager, she won an amateur talent show at Harlem's storied Apollo Theater, and a star was born. She moved into the house in Queens with her husband, bassist Ray Brown, in 1949. The couple divorced in 1953, but Fitzgerald stayed put until 1956.

- **Milt Hinton** (173–05 113th Avenue): A resident of Queens for 50 years until his death in 2000, Hinton was a bassist and sideman for a staggering number of artists (as a studio musician, he appeared on 1,174 recordings), including Cab Calloway, Benny Goodman, Ben Webster, and neighbors Louis Armstrong and Count Basie.

- **Cootie Williams** (175–19 Linden Boulevard): From 1947 to 1953, this star trumpet player of the Duke Ellington Band lived in a three-story Tudor-style house that featured a prominent fairy tale-inspired turret. Another notable musician lived there in the 1960s: Godfather of Soul James Brown.

## Royal Flushing

The Flushing Cemetery in Flushing, Queens, is the final resting place for two prominent jazz trumpeters: Louis Armstrong (1901–71) and "Crown Prince of Bop" Dizzy Gillespie (1917–93).

*Fats Waller plays the boogie-woogie.*

# You Know You're a New Yorker When...

- You're living in a 350-square-foot studio apartment that costs $2,000 a month…and you think it's a fantastic deal.
- Your navigational directions are east, west, uptown, and downtown.
- You've never been to the Empire State Building, the Statue of Liberty, or Times Square on New Year's Eve, but you have seen Ground Zero at midnight, and you've walked the Highline.
- You say "the city" but mean "Manhattan."
- You sprint to catch the subway even when you're not in a hurry.
- You consider yourself multilingual if you can curse in more than one language.
- Westchester is considered "upstate."

*The 9/11 memorial at Ground Zero lights up the New York City skyline.*

# Manhattanhenge

*Want to see a perfect sunset? Twice a year, you can get your wish right here in Manhattan.*

### Let the Sun Shine

Most of the time, the tall buildings in Manhattan block the sunset. But twice a year, above 14th Street, the sun aligns with the streets' east–west grid pattern and sets perfectly between the buildings. It lasts only about 15 minutes, but it's so striking that people stop on the streets to watch. As solar rays light up the towering buildings, a glowing orange light filters along the streets.

The reflection off the buildings also scatters the sunshine, sending bright light along the north–south avenues. Because the phenomenon resembles sunsets seen at England's mysterious Stonehenge ruins,

Neil deGrasse Tyson, an astrophysicist at the American Museum of Natural History in Manhattan, calls it "Manhattanhenge."

## Perfection…Almost

Stonehenge was built by the ancient Celtic Druids to mark the exact moment of the spring and fall equinoxes, when the sun rises and sets due east and due west of true north. But Manhattan's street grid was established in 1811 for efficiency, not science, so it's slightly off center—it's turned 28.9 degrees from true east and west, to be exact. As a result, the city's "equinoxes" occur on different days each year. Usually, the dates are in late May and mid-July. But if you miss the exact dates, not to worry. The day before or after Manhattanhenge also creates a celestial glow—it's not quite as magnificent, but still pretty good.

According to Tyson, who calculates the dates each year for the museum's planetarium, the best way to see Manhattanhenge is this:

> Position yourself as far east in Manhattan as possible, but ensure that when you look west across the avenues you can still see New Jersey. Clear cross streets include 14th, 23rd, 34th, 42nd, 57th, and several streets adjacent to them. The Empire State Building and the Chrysler Building render 34th Street and 42nd Streets especially striking vistas.

*Manhattenhenge occurs only twice a year.*

# The Library Inspires New York

During the Great Depression, Mayor Fiorello La Guardia named the stone lions outside the New York Public Library Patience and Fortitude, to remind New Yorkers that they could survive the economic disaster. In addition, the library ran a store in its basement, offering groceries, food, tobacco, and clothing at reasonable prices.

*Patience stands guard outside the New York Public Library.*

# "They Got Punked!"

*Even gritty New Yorkers are gullible. Here, we'll take a trip through some of the silliest hoaxes ever perpetrated on a city (supposedly) full of skeptics.*

*Astronomer Sir John Herschel was a victim of the* Sun's *hoax too.*

## The Great Moon Hoax

**Perpetrator:** The *New York Sun* newspaper

**Story:** The paper printed its first issue in 1833, and by 1835, it was looking for a circulation boost. So to drum up interest, editors announced the upcoming publication of six articles covering renowned British astronomer Sir John Herschel's fantastic new "discoveries" of life on the Moon: forests and seas, cranes and pelicans, herds of bison and goats, flocks of blue unicorns, sapphire temples with 70-foot pillars—even a race of batlike humanoid creatures. According to the *Sun,* the articles would be reprinted from the *Edinburgh Journal of Science.*

The day the first article appeared, *Sun* sales were 15,000; by the sixth day, they were over 19,000, the highest of any New York paper of the time. Other newspapers, racing to catch up, claimed to have the "original" *Edinburgh Journal* articles too, but they actually just reprinted the *Sun*'s stories.

**Exposed!** There were no *Edinburgh Journal* articles. In fact, that journal had gone out of business several years earlier. And Herschel, perhaps the most eminent astronomer of his time, was totally ignorant of the hoax (and then amused by it until he got sick of answering questions about Moon men). The articles were reportedly written by *Sun* reporter Richard Adams Locke. The *Sun* never formally admitted the deception, but it did publish a column speculating that a hoax was "possible." Regardless, the paper got what it wanted and circulation remained high.

## The 140-Year-Old Hot Dog Hoax

**Perpetrator:** The Coney Island History Project

**Story:** In 2009 and 2010, the Astroland amusement park at Coney Island was being demolished to make room for new games and rides. On Wednesday, February 24, 2010, the old kitchen building of the block-long Feltman's restaurant on Surf Avenue was scheduled to go. (Charles Feltman was credited with the invention of the hot dog in 1874, and also with hiring the young

*Two illustrations that appeared in the 1835* New York Sun *depict "life" on the Moon.*

14

*The "140-year-old" hot dog*

Nathan Handwerker, who eventually struck out on his own and opened the legendary Nathan's Famous hot dog stand.)

According to CNN, which got the story from a local TV station, during demolition, an amateur archaeologist unearthed an ice-encrusted object that he claimed was an original Feltman's hot dog…140 years old. Officials of the Coney Island History Project swore that the dog, the bun, and an original receipt from Feltman's had been preserved by the ice, and they immediately put the thawing relic on display. CNN, Grub Street (a New York food blog), and thousands of Tweeters bought it.

**Exposed!** On February 26, a spokesperson for the History Project admitted that it was all a publicity stunt in the "grand tradition of Coney Island ballyhoo." The point? To get people out to Coney Island to see the Project's exhibit about Feltman's. It was a success—hundreds of people hurried out to Coney Island to see the show.

## The Central Park International Airport Hoax

**Perpetrator:** The Manhattan Airport Foundation (MAF)

**Story:** On July 21, 2009, the Manhattan Airport Foundation (MAF) ran an Internet posting with an unusual idea: to bulldoze Central Park and turn it into an airport. The MAF called for "the immediate development of a viable and centrally located international air transportation hub in New York City."

**Where?** Central Park. Strawberry Fields would be replanted inside the new terminal, the Tavern on the Green restaurant could move to the food court, and the Central Park Zoo would be relocated. The *Huffington Post* ran the story on its front page.

**Exposed!** Who is the Manhattan Airport Foundation? No one knows. The group has a website and claimed to have offices on the 58th floor of the Woolworth Building (which has only 57 floors). According to MAF's website, a petition to destroy the park in favor of the airport got 19,000 signatures.

*Strawberry Fields still stands. Thankfully, the plan to bulldoze Central Park and build an airport in Manhattan was a hoax.*

15

# There Goes the Neighborhood: The Bronx

*The Bronx is the only borough of New York City that isn't an island. Want to know more? Read on!*

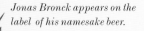

*Jonas Bronck appears on the label of his namesake beer.*

- The **Bronx** was named for the nearby Bronx River, which itself was named for Jonas Bronck, an immigrant from Sweden who settled in the area in the 17th century.

- The town of **Spuyten Duyvil**, a wooded neighborhood near the Hudson and Harlem Rivers, also gets its name from a body of water: the Spuyten Duyvil Creek. Depending on how you pronounce them, the words mean "devil's whirlpool" or "spite the devil" in Dutch. (It's unclear why the Dutch had such a low opinion of the creek.)

- New Yorkers can thank Jordan L. Mott, who opened an ironworks in the Bronx in the mid-1800s, for the neighborhood of **Mott Haven**. When the previous owner of the land—Gouverneur Morris II, who'd called the area Morristown—was asked if he minded Mott changing the neighborhood's name, he quipped, "I don't care...while he is about it, he might as well change the Harlem River to the Jordan."

- **Tremont** got its name from a 19th-century mailman who combined three (*tre*) neighborhoods in west-central Bronx: Fairmount, Mount Hope, and Mount Eden.

- Between 1968 and 1970, the City of New York built a housing project of 15,372 units on 300 acres of filled marshland in the northeastern Bronx.

*Bronx-born Jordan L. Mott, for whom the neighborhood Mott Haven is named, appears in this 1857 painting:* Men of Progress. *He sits at the table (second from the left) and is surrounded by other influential American inventors and scientists.*

*The Bronx today*

It was one of the largest housing projects in the country and had room for about 60,000 people. Today, it's called **Co-op City**, and if it weren't part of the Bronx, it would be the tenth-largest city in the state of New York.

*The Bronx Traveling Library, founded in 1928, made books available to those who did not have access to a permanent library.*

# New York on $0 a Day

*New York is one of the most expensive cities in the world, but there are lots of things to do and see for free.*

- You'll have to get them in advance—and sometimes get on a waiting list—but TV shows with studio audiences that tape in New York offer free tickets. Some of them include *The View*, *Saturday Night Live*, *The Tonight Show*, and *The Daily Show*.

- Can't get tickets? Get up early, make a homemade sign, and stand outside the glass windows behind the hosts on *Today*.

- Lots of New York City museums offer free admission on Friday evenings. The list includes the Museum of Modern Art, the Museum of the Moving Image, the New York Historical Society, the Whitney Museum of American Art, the Bronx Museum of the Arts, and the American Folk Art Museum.

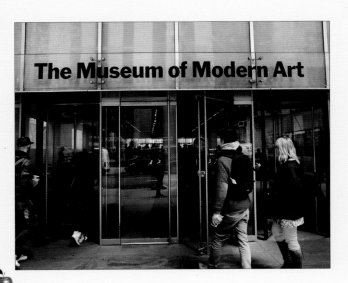

*The Museum of Modern Art is just one of many cultural attractions in the city that offer free Friday night admission.*

- Central Park—all 843 acres (1.3 square miles) of it—is free and available for walking around, exploring, taking a nap, or throwing a Frisbee. The Central Park Conservancy also offers free walking tours, and information on the park's history and plant life. The summer months bring Shakespeare in the Park. Presented by the Public Theater, these are full productions of Shakespeare plays staged in Central Park by world-class actors.

- From June to August, there are nighttime outdoor classic movie screenings in Bryant Park. The grounds open at 5 p.m. (thousands bring blankets and picnics), and the show starts at sunset.

- You don't *have* to buy anything at the city's fancy world-famous department stores, such as Saks Fifth Avenue, Bergdorf Goodman, or FAO Schwartz—you can gawk or live vicariously.

*The Unisphere towers over Flushing Meadows in Queens.*

- Almost every weekday afternoon during the school year, students from the Juilliard School put on free classical concerts at Lincoln Center.

- The city operates a program called Big Apple Greeters, which matches up volunteer tour guides with visitors based on common interests. Visitors then get a guided tour of New York City tailor-made to what they're most interested in.

- Flushing Meadows–Corona Park in Queens is bigger than Central Park. For free, you can see the Unisphere, take a walk around Meadow Lake, and walk by two of the country's most famous sports complexes: Citi Field (home of the Mets) and the U.S. National Tennis Center (home of the U.S. Open).

- The Strand bookstore at the corner of 12th and Broadway houses 18 miles of books. It's also a hot spot for celebrity sightings: Patti Smith, Robert Pattinson, Orlando Bloom, and others have all been caught shopping there. Browsing and people-watching are free.

*The Strand bookstore is a great place to read, shop, or people-watch.*

- The Downtown Boathouse offers free kayaking lessons and tours of New York Harbor on the weekends and weekday evenings between May and October. Classes meet at Pier 40, Pier 96, and 72nd Street and are all first come, first served.

# Gentleman Jim

Born in California, James "Gentleman Jim" Corbett—famous for knocking out boxing champ John L. Sullivan in 1892—lived the second half of his life in Bayside, Queens. Corbett moved to Bayside in 1902 at the age of 36, and lived there until his death in 1933. After his boxing career ended, Corbett performed in vaudeville, and some low-budget movies, and wrote his life story, which was later turned into a movie that starred Errol Flynn. A *Bayside Times* writer once described Corbett's elegant style, which contributed to his nickname: "In the winter, he would have on a long black Chesterfield coat with a velvet collar, a derby hat, white shirt with a beautiful tie, a gleaming diamond stickpin, grey fawn gloves, a white scarf and, of course, grey spats, which were in vogue in those days."

*Today Show hosts Hoda Kotb and Carson Daly enjoy some refreshments on the set.*

*The Downtown Boathouse offers free kayaking lessons.*

# Flushed with Pride

*What exactly flows under the streets that New Yorkers walk on every day?  Read on (and flush twice).*

## Flushing, New York

New York became America's largest—and, some say, most civilized—city in 1835, but its sanitation system was way behind the times. Most homes, even the most expensive ones, had privies out back. That meant waste fell into a hole in the ground, and when the hole was full, someone covered it with dirt and dug another hole.

Pigs roamed Manhattan, eating up garbage and sewage on city streets. By the late 1800s, after several outbreaks of water-borne diseases, it became obvious that something needed to be done about all the sewage.

The city's first two wastewater treatment facilities were located in Brooklyn and Queens, and in 1906 the city established the Metropolitan Sewerage Commission to handle municipal waste. But the system was overwhelmed by New York's ever-growing population. By 1910 about 700 million gallons of raw sewage flowed into the city's rivers every day, and *Sunday Magazine* reported, "the Hudson River was so dirty that it could barely support fish."

The Sewerage Commission responded by adding new treatment plants and upgrading others, and today, New York City's wastewater treatment plants handle more than a billion gallons of sewage per day through almost 7,500 miles of sewer pipes.

Still, it's not enough. As New Yorkers know, when it rains, raw sewage often threatens to back up through storm drains and into the subway. When that happens, the city's wastewater system does what it was built to do: It still discharges overflow into the East River, the Hudson River, and New York Harbor.

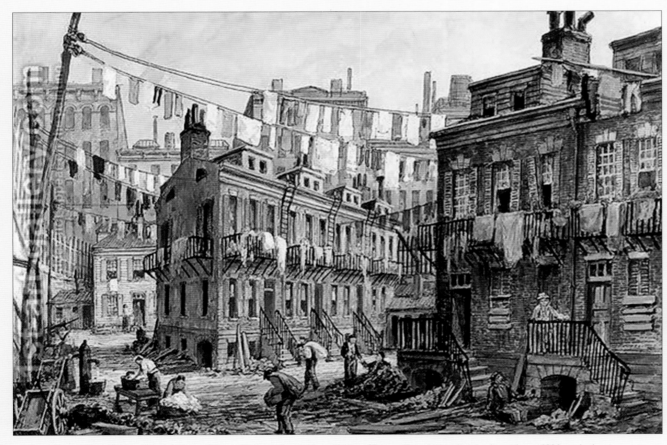

*It took a while for New Yorkers to catch on to the importance of sanitation. Here, garbage litters Baxter Street in an 1880s painting.*

## Aw, Rats!

But aside from the obvious, what's really down in the sewers?

- One report estimated that there are 500 rats per mile of sewer pipes. (Another thought there were more rats in New York City than people, but that's never been proven.) Most of them are *Rattus norvegicus*, or the common brown sewer rat, which can grow to weigh about two pounds and has been known to attack humans, even in broad daylight.

- Despite the number of urban legends, officially, there are no alligators in the city's sewers. But during the 1920s and '30s, the *New York Times* was full of stories about alligators running wild in the city. Still, only one of the stories actually reported an alligator near a sewer. It's more likely that any gators found in New York City or its surrounding waterways came from some aboveground source: aquarium escapees, lost shipping cargo,

and so on. Plus, alligators are warm-weather creatures, and New York winters are too cold for the animals to survive.

- Animals fall into the sewers all the time, and smaller animals undoubtedly get flushed down. Most of them are dead before the whoosh, but some make it out alive, including turtles, fish, and at least one small and extremely lucky dog.

- Sewer workers have fished out guns, knives, games, mattresses, Christmas decorations, electronics, jewelry, telephones, silverware, auto parts, tires, dead bodies, and a glass eye.

*What might you find in the sewers of New York?*

# Mad About *Mad Men*

*Few TV shows in recent history have made New York City look as sleek and sophisticated as* Mad Men *has. Here's some random trivia about Don Draper and the gang.*

- In 2008 *Mad Men* was nominated for (and won) an Emmy for Outstanding Drama Series, the first basic cable show to receive that distinction.

- In real life, Talia Balsam—who plays Mona, Roger Sterling's ex-wife—is married to John Slattery...who plays Roger Sterling.

- Although the show is well known for its realistic portrayal of the sexist 1960s, many of its primary writers are women.

*Inset: Jon Hamm and January Jones star in* Mad Men.

- The actors on *Mad Men* smoke only nicotine-free cigarettes. In California, where the show is filmed, it's illegal to smoke real cigarettes indoors, including inside sound stages.

- Kiernan Shipka, who plays Sally Draper, wasn't allowed to watch the show at first—she was just eight when it premiered in 2007. Her mother prescreened each episode and showed her only the scenes she was in.

- In 2009, during the third season of *Mad Men*, President Barack Obama sent creator Matthew Weiner a letter saying how much he enjoyed the show.

# Weird News

*New Yorkers do the darndest things.*

*Playwright Paul Walker (left) directs actors Laoisa Sexton and Sean Gormley in a men's room in Central Park.*

### Trash Pile

After the blizzards of 2010–11, trash sat on city streets for weeks and irritated everyone from Staten Island to the Bronx. But it turned out to be a lucky break for Vangelis Kapatos of Manhattan, who, in January 2011, tried to kill himself by jumping out of a window on West 45th Street. Fortunately, about 100 bags of trash at the curb below broke his fall. "He landed on a garbage pile," said one city official. "That's the only reason he's alive." Kapatos

*Above: In 2008 playwright Paul Walker staged a play in a Central Park restroom like this one.*

wasn't injured, and his family took him to Bellevue for psychiatric evaluation.

## Give His Regards to the Bathroom

In 2008 Irish playwright Paul Walker staged an unusual production: His play *Ladies & Gents* was performed in a bathroom in Central Park. Why? According to Walker, he wanted to take the audience "out of their comfort zone." The play was a thriller about a sex scandal in 1950s Ireland, and it was performed in two 20-minute parts: one in the ladies' room, and one in the men's; audience members switched bathrooms to see how the story ended. (Portable, working toilets were stationed outside for the public, since the facilities were occupied.) In its review of the show, the *New York Times* said, "The cast members sell the gimmick perfectly."

## Excess Baggage

In January 2011, Columbia University researcher Edward Hall III arrived at JFK Airport to catch a flight to the West Coast... and realized he'd forgotten his picture ID. He tried to get help from one of the United Airlines desk agents, explaining that he "really needed to get to San Francisco." When she refused to allow him to board without his ID, Hall took matters into his own hands: He jumped over the ticket counter and dove onto the baggage conveyor belt...which carried him through the airport and deposited him on the tarmac. Airport personnel detained him, and when police arrived to take him into custody, he explained, "I just wanted to make my flight."

# Subway Facts

*The Y-cut token*

- The New York City subway is the largest subway system in the world, with 659 miles of track, 468 stations, and 6,290 subway cars.

- Riding the subway reduces carbon emissions by 80 percent per mile, compared to a single occupancy car.

- About 4.5 million people ride the subway each weekday.

- Busiest subway station: Times Square, with 58 million passengers per year.

- Subway tokens were introduced on July 2, 1953. The iconic Y-cut was designed to make them identifiable by touch in your pocket. The Y-cut in subway tokens was removed in 1980 because lint caught in it was clogging machines.

- The Metrocard was introduced on January 6, 1994. The last token machines were removed on December 11, 1997.

- In 1985 the Metropolitan Transit Authority (MTA) started the Arts for Transit program, which has commissioned 125 works of art (murals, mosaics, and sculptures) for subway stations. The Music Under New York program also pays about 100 professional musicians to play in the subway stations, and yes, they have to audition—the ones who are there officially, at least.

*Commuters rush past a mural inside the Times Square subway station.*

# The Skinny on Skyscrapers

*New York's decision to build skyward was based on necessity and technological invention…and driven by a heavy dose of ego.*

## Five-Story Limit

By the 1820s, New York was the economic capital of the country. The city's growing businesses needed office space, but even back then, midtown Manhattan real estate was pricey. So owners wanted taller buildings—one way to get more usable space onto a small, expensive lot. But building high presented several problems.

The most obvious was gravity. Climbing up and down more than five or six flights of stairs made everyday business tasks—or just getting to the office—difficult. Plus, many of the practical needs for a skyscraper hadn't been developed yet: reliable central heating, indoor plumbing, and lighting systems.

*Manhattan, as shown in this 1827 painting, was a lot shorter before skyscrapers.*

And then there was the problem of the foundation. In the early 19th century, anyone who wanted to construct a building more than 10 stories high had to use the same technology that was around during the time of the pyramids: a huge foundation with thick walls that could support the weight of the building. A 16-story building built of brick or stone, for instance, required walls that were at least six feet thick. To soar 20 stories or more, a building would have needed an enormous foundation that might not fit into a narrow midtown lot.

And the walls would have to be so thick that they'd take up most of the square footage on the lower floors—there would be hardly any room left in it for office space. Tall commercial buildings seemed completely impractical, so in the mid-1800s, the Manhattan skyline boasted very few buildings more than five stories high.

## Up, Up, Up, and Away

That didn't last long, however. In 1852 inventor Elisha Graves Otis from

*Elisha Graves Otis*

Yonkers created the first safety brake for elevators. The elevator had been around for centuries, evolving from crude pulley systems to ones that worked with hydraulics, but they carried mostly freight because they were dangerous and difficult to control. Otis's brake, which prevented the elevator from falling if a cable snapped, made them safe for passengers. Five years later, Otis installed New York's first elevator in a department store on Broadway. It worked so well that its architects began to think vertically. By 1875 New York developers had begun constructing 10-story office buildings with elevators. The late 1800s also saw improvements in the electric light bulb, central heating, plumbing, and the telephone. Together, these amenities made it at least possible to construct an extremely high building.

But the foundation was still a problem—one that an Englishman named Henry Bessemer and an American, William Kelly, were each trying to solve. Steel was a strong, light metal that could eliminate the need for thick walls, but during the mid-19th century, making steel required an enormous amount of coal to heat the metal. The process was extremely costly and time-consuming, and steel was so expensive at the time that forks and knives made of the metal cost more than those made of gold.

But then, in 1856, Bessemer (who later bought out his competitor Kelly) figured out how to mass-produce steel by using a furnace that blew air through molten iron. The air added oxygen to the burning process, and oxidization removed impurities from the iron; all that remained was high-quality steel. The Bessemer process needed less fuel, and tons of steel could be produced quickly. Prices tumbled, and steel suddenly became available for building projects.

## The First Skyscrapers

By the 1880s, New York's buildings were being constructed in an entirely new way. Much of Manhattan rests on granite rock, so crews dug down to that bedrock, which wouldn't shift. On that solid foundation, builders set footings—large concrete and

steel pads that spread out to absorb the weight of an enormous structure.

Vertical steel columns were then attached to the footings, connected to each other by horizontal steel girders. Diagonal beams could be riveted to the girders and columns for extra support. The columns, girders, and beams formed a rigid steel cage that was strong but also lightweight. To keep that light cage from swaying in the force of strong winds, vertical concrete cores were installed. Sometimes the cores anchored the center of the building around the elevator shafts; other times, concrete was poured around the vertical columns near the building's perimeter. Either way, the heavy concrete helped stabilize the structure and anchor it against wind pressure.

These steel frameworks were so strong and absorbed so much of a building's weight that there was no longer a need for thick outer walls. Instead, the outer walls became known as "curtain walls," because they weren't supporting the structure and hung like curtains on the inner frame. They could then be fitted with glass that brought in light and views.

## This Means War!

Most people agree that the first

*This view of Manhattan in the early 1900s shows two of the city's most famous skyscrapers: the Woolworth Building (rear left tower) and the Singer Building (tower to its right).*

*The triangular Flatiron Building opened on Fifth Avenue in 1902.*

skyscraper in New York was the 100-foot-tall Tower Building, which opened in 1889 on a narrow lot at 50 Broadway. A decade later, the Park Row Building became the tallest office building in the world, rising to 391 feet.

In those early days, many New Yorkers worried about skyscrapers toppling—especially when the triangular Flatiron Building opened on Fifth Avenue in 1902.

The Flatiron was 285 feet high and only six feet wide at its narrowest point. Its shape seemed so unstable that gamblers placed bets on when it would fall. (It's still there.)

As the city got used to skyscrapers—and they proved to be safe—"height wars" pushed buildings skyward. Owning one of the world's tallest buildings wasn't just a great advertising tool—it was also a status symbol. Retail millionaire F. W.

Woolworth decided that he wanted to own the tallest, most beautiful skyscraper in the world. In 1910 he commissioned the Woolworth Building. It opened three years later and rose to a staggering 760 feet, designed in a Gothic style that gave it the nickname "the Cathedral of Commerce." In 1931 the Woolworth Building was eclipsed by the even taller Empire State Building. At more than 1,200 feet high, the Empire State Building remained the world's tallest building for more than 40 years until the World Trade Center climbed 100 feet higher. Since the 1970s, other cities have built even taller skyscrapers—today, the world's tallest building is the Burj Khalifa in Dubai (2,717 feet). But it all started in New York.

# Opening Lines

*Here are some great openings from some quintessentially New York books. How many have you read?*

"It was a queer, sultry summer, the summer they electrocuted the Rosenbergs, and I didn't know what I was doing in New York."

**—Sylvia Plath,** *The Bell Jar*

"On the first day of my teaching career, I was almost fired for eating the sandwich of a high school boy."

**—Frank McCourt,** *Teacher Man*

"On some nights, New York is as hot as Bangkok."

**—Saul Bellow,** *The Victim*

"My biggest problem is my brother, Farley Drexel Hatcher. Everybody calls him Fudge. I feel sorry for him if he's going to grow up with a name like Fudge, but I don't say a word. It's none of my business."

**—Judy Blume,** *Tales of a Fourth Grade Nothing*

*Inset: Salvatore Corsitto (left) and Marlon Brando appear in the 1972 film adaptation of* The Godfather.

"Amerigo Bonasera sat in New York Criminal Court Number 3 and waited for justice; vengeance on the men who had so cruelly hurt his daughter, who had tried to dishonor her."

**—Mario Puzo,** *The Godfather*

*Above: The spire of the Woolworth Building pierces the sky.*
*Facing page: The Empire State Building glows just before sunset.*

# New York Food from A to P

*A smorgasbord of some of New York's favorite edibles and grazing grounds.*

**Amy's Bread:** When your upscale bistro's breadbasket has a black-olive twist or a raisin-fennel roll in it, it's probably from Amy's. In 1992 Amy Scherber and her five employees started selling handmade specialty breads from a storefront on 9th Avenue. Today she has over 150 workers and three retail locations—one of them in Chelsea Market, where the bread baking is done behind a glass wall. Wave to the bakers!

**Buffalo Wings:** These chicken wings, prepared with spicy sauce and served with celery sticks and blue cheese dressing, were invented by Teressa Bellissimo at the Anchor Bar in Buffalo in 1964. Since then, they've become essential bar food all over the country.

**Chopped Liver:** New York didn't invent it—so what? From Brooklyn to the Bronx, chopped liver is as New York as the Yankees. Ingredients: sautéed chicken livers, schmaltz (chicken fat), hard-boiled eggs, salt, pepper, and onions.

**Danish:** Actually it's danish *pastry*, but in New York it's just plain "danish" with a lowercase "d." Cheese danish, prune danish, maybe cherry, pecan, or cinnamon raisin. With a paper cup of coffee, the breakfast of New York champions.

**Entenmann's Baked Goods:** In 1898 William Entenmann opened a bakery in Brooklyn and delivered door-to-door. Locals loved his layer cake, doughnuts, pies, and crumb coffee cake—but it wasn't until 1951, when the bakery started supplying supermarkets, that *all* New Yorkers had the opportunity to get hooked. Entenmann's is still going strong, with more than 100 products.

**Fairway Market:** The grocery chain opened in 1976 on the Upper West Side, undercutting the competition with great prices on produce, cheese, and baked goods—and won a following so devoted that the place was (and still is) jam-packed night and day. Branches have opened in Manhattan, Brooklyn,

*Some artists turn New York hot dogs into ornaments and earrings.*

Long Island, and Westchester, with more stores in the works.

**God's Love We Deliver:** This service was founded in 1986 by Ganga Stone and Jane Best to take nutritionally appropriate meals to AIDS patients. Restaurants contributed food, volunteers helped cook and deliver, and philanthropists gave funds. By 2009 the group had delivered its 10 millionth meal.

**Hebrew National Kosher Meats:** In 1905 Isadore Pinckowitz began making high-quality kosher franks and sausages on the Lower East Side, first selling to delis and the (Jewish) Waldbaum's grocery chain, then to supermarkets. His meats contained no by-products and no artificial colors or flavors, and the 1965 slogan said it all: "We Answer to a Higher Authority."

**Ice Cream, Häagen-Dazs:** Despite the "Danish" name, this is a born-and-bred New York product. In 1960 Bronx resident

*Even puppies love New York hot dogs.*

Reuben Mattus took his popular "super-premium" homemade ice cream (which he'd been selling to local restaurants), gave it an exotic foreign name, packed it in fancy cartons, and started a multimillion-dollar company. Originally, he offered only vanilla, chocolate, and coffee, but the company carries 25 flavors today.

**Junior's Cheesecake:** The signature dessert of Junior's Restaurant in Brooklyn. In the 1950s, people traveled from all over the city for a slice; it was as famous as the Brooklyn Dodgers. In 1973 six judges unanimously chose it "Champion Cheesecake" in *New York* magazine's cheesecake contest.

**Korean Groceries:** By the 1970s, Korean-run groceries were well established in most neighborhoods, open 24/7, selling everything from fresh produce and flowers to soda and snacks. They became convenient alternatives to supermarkets, but it was their

*Knotty New York pretzels*

lavish "salad bars"—the first ones in a deli setting—stocked with everything from salad to dumplings to mac and cheese that really pulled in the customers.

**Li-Lac Chocolates:** New York's oldest handmade chocolates, still prepared with the same recipes used by original owner George Demetrious when he opened his shop on Christopher Street in Greenwich Village in 1923. The store has since moved to Eighth Avenue in the Village, and there's another one in Grand Central's Market Hall.

**Mayonnaise, Hellmann's Blue Ribbon:** After Richard Hellmann opened a deli in Manhattan in 1905, his customers begged to buy tubs of his wife's homemade mayo. Finally, in 1912, he began to manufacture and bottle it in Astoria, Queens. He gave up the deli in 1917 to plunge full-time into the mayonnaise biz.

**Nesselrode Pie:** Nineteenth-century Russian Count Nesselrode lent his name to this pie that was popular in

*An Elvis impersonator grabs a pretzel in New York.*

New York City in the 1940s and '50s, especially at Christmas. Now as rare as baked Alaska, it featured candied fruits folded into light, fluffy, rum-flavored Bavarian cream that was spooned into a piecrust and topped with chocolate shavings.

**Onion Board (Pletzel):** A sort of eastern European focaccia made of yeast-raised dough flattened to about 12 by 15 inches, topped with sautéed onions and poppy seeds, and baked until golden brown. New York's pletzel mecca is Kossar's bakery on Grand Street in Manhattan, which has handcrafted its bagels, bialys, and pletzels since 1936.

**Pretzel, Soft:** The authentic New York soft pretzel, bought from a street vendor, is about eight inches across and is usually topped with a squiggle of neon-yellow mustard. It's New York City road food, grabbed on the run, guaranteed to tide you over until your next meal.

# Bedbugs, Bedbugs

*Whatcha gonna do when they come for you?*

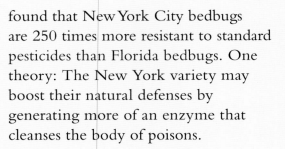

- According to entomologists at the American Museum of Natural History, 20 percent of New Yorkers had bedbugs in their homes during the 2009–11 infestation epidemic.

- Latin name for bedbugs: *Cimex lectularius.*

- Bedbugs are most active at night. Why? Because they live off of human blood, and that's when people are easiest to bite.

- Bedbugs are only a few millimeters long, and as thin as a business card. So even if walls look sealed, bedbugs can usually find a way in.

- With hundreds of thousands of apartments so close together in New York City, an infestation can spread quickly as bugs travel through cable conduits, heaters, and drop ceilings, or simply by scurrying across hallways.

- Notable locations infested with bedbugs: former president Bill Clinton's Harlem offices, the Metropolitan Opera House, the Waldorf-Astoria hotel, Fox News headquarters, Time Warner headquarters, *Elle* magazine, the Empire State Building, and flagship stores of Nike, Victoria's Secret, and Abercrombie & Fitch.

- Number of New York City bedbug complaints in 2006: 4,600. Number in 2009: more than 9,200.

- The bugs can live and breed for weeks without water, and for months without food.

- A University of Massachusetts study found that New York City bedbugs are 250 times more resistant to standard pesticides than Florida bedbugs. One theory: The New York variety may boost their natural defenses by generating more of an enzyme that cleanses the body of poisons.

- According to a poll by *Glamour*, 57 percent of guys would go home with a girl who admitted to having bedbugs.

- In 2011 the Animal Planet cable network began soliciting stories for a show about people with harrowing bedbug-related stories. The prize: free extermination.

- Protesting Teamsters used to picket union-unfriendly businesses while carrying a giant inflatable rat. In 2010 some switched to a giant bedbug.

*Not everybody hates bedbugs: Bedbug lovers protest in New York City.*

- Estimated cost of fumigating an apartment building for bedbugs: $70,000.

- Bedbug bites start out painless but eventually turn into large, itchy welts. Unlike a flea bite, they lack a red center spot (that's how you know what bit you). On the bright side, bedbugs are not known to spread disease from human to human.

- Removal and prevention tip: Steam killers and liquid nitrogen treatments kill only the bedbugs they come into direct contact with. Common, over-the-counter aerosols don't work, either—experts say those mostly just make the bugs scurry elsewhere. Exterminators typically have to use pesticides or extreme heat to kill bedbugs.

- If you think you're at risk for bedbugs, seal all cracks and crevices, including cable conduits; vacuum your carpets, mattresses, and other cloth furniture thoroughly; and wash all your clothes, towels, and linens in hot water, and then dry them on the highest setting.

- Despite the widely covered 2009–11 bedbug epidemic, New York City isn't the most afflicted place in the United States. According to the extermination company Orkin, Chicago is #1. New York isn't even in the top 15.

# Govern-mental

Until the mid-1980s, New Yorkers could tell what borough they were in based on the colors of the street signs:

- **Queens:** White background with blue lettering.
- **Manhattan and Staten Island:** Yellow background with black lettering.
- **Bronx:** Blue background with white lettering.
- **Brooklyn:** Black background with white lettering.

But in 1985, the federal government said that green was the easiest color for the eye to see, so by law, all American street signs had to be green with white lettering. New York City made the change. Then, in 2010, came yet another street-sign initiative mandated by the federal government, this time to convert any signs currently in all capital letters into lowercase with initial caps for each new word. According to the Department of Transportation, the lowercase letters are easier to read, so they will decrease the number of accidents. With more than 250,000 street signs in the five boroughs, each costing $110 to replace, the expense is estimated at over $27 million. New York and other cities protested, saying, "While the mixed-case words might be easier to read, the amount of improvement in legibility did not justify the cost." The feds refused to relent, but did give cities until 2018 to make the change.

# Destroying New York

*Whether blowing it up, burning it down, or covering it in marshmallow goo, the movies really seem to have it in for New York City.*

*Ben Affleck in* Armageddon

### Escape from New York (1981)

**Plot:** The United States is awash in crime, and Manhattan is a wasteland and maximum-security prison isolated from the rest of the country. When a hijacking lands the U.S. president there, a convict and former soldier known as Snake (Kurt Russell) is given 22 hours to find the president and earn his freedom.

*Kurt Russell looks tough in* Escape from New York.

### Armageddon (1998)

**Plot:** Flaming meteorites flatten the Chrysler Building and Grand Central Station in the opening sequence, and a *really big* meteorite is on track to destroy Earth in 18 days unless Bruce Willis and his drilling crew can intervene in time.

### Independence Day (1996)

**Plot:** Alien spaceships blow up the Empire State Building and then attack other major cities. Governments around the globe join forces to fight the alien menace. (Fortunately, Will Smith is on their side.)

*An alien vessel looms over Manhattan in a scene from* Independence Day.

## Ghostbusters (1984)

**Plot:** New York City is being overrun by poltergeists after a gateway to another dimension opens up in Manhattan and threatens the world. A quartet of ragtag exorcists (Dan Aykroyd, Bill Murray, Harold Ramis, and Ernie Hudson) goes on the hunt and battles, among other beasts, an enormous Stay Puft Marshmallow Man who stomps the Holy Trinity Lutheran Church on Central Park West into sticky rubble.

## The Day After Tomorrow (2004)

**Plot:** In this movie about climate change and its aftermath, rising tides swamp the city, which then freezes over. A small group led by a young man named Sam (Jake Gyllenhaal) survives by burning books in the main branch of the New York Public Library.

*Actress Emmy Rossum gets caught in a storm in a scene from* The Day After Tomorrow.

*The Ghostbusters in action*

# New York Tidbits

- Broadway is also called Highway 9.

- In the early 1890s, 100 European starlings were released in Central Park, the first in North America. Today, 200 million starlings live throughout the United States.

- When the United States became a nation in 1776, the tallest structure in NYC was Trinity Church.

- In 1848 Lucretia Mott and Elizabeth Cady Stanton held the first women's-rights convention, in Seneca Falls in upstate New York.

- Total manpower used to cut 20 miles of tunnels for the NYC subway: 7,700 men.

- Montauk, Long Island, is home to Deep Hollow Ranch, the oldest cattle ranch in the United States.

*Deep Hollow Ranch*

# Uncle John's Page of Lists

*Some random information from the BRI's trivia files.*

## 4 Bodies of Water That Border New York State

1. Atlantic Ocean
2. Lake Ontario
3. Lake Erie
4. Lake Champlain

## 3 Husbands of Jennifer Lopez

1. Ojani Noa
2. Cris Judd
3. Marc Anthony

## 7 Original *SNL* Cast Members

1. Dan Aykroyd
2. John Belushi
3. Gilda Radner
4. Chevy Chase
5. Jane Curtin
6. Laraine Newman
7. Garrett Morris

*Jennifer Lopez has married (from left) Ojani Noa, Marc Anthony, and Cris Judd.*

## 2 Ivy League Universities in New York State

1. Cornell
2. Columbia

## 4 Stadiums That the New York Jets Have Called Home

1. The Polo Grounds
2. Shea Stadium
3. Giants Stadium
4. The Meadowlands (now MetLife)

## 4 New York Newspapers That No Longer Exist

1. *The New York Mirror*
2. *The New York Sun*
3. *The Brooklyn Times Union*
4. *The Herald Tribune*

## 1 Official State Muffin

1. Apple

## 1 Coney Island Roller Coaster Still in Operation (opened 1927)

1. The Cyclone

## 2 Items of Clothing Required at the Great New York State Fair, held annually in Syracuse

1. A shirt
2. Footwear

## 5 Boroughs in New York City (From the Most to the Least Populous)

1. Brooklyn (2,592,149)
2. Queens (2,296,175)
3. Manhattan (1,626,159)
4. Bronx (1,418,733)
5. Staten Island (472,621)

*Riders brave the famous Cyclone roller coaster at Coney Island.*

# So You Think You Know New York City?

*A few facts that even seasoned New Yorkers might not know.*

- There are more than 2,000 bridges in New York City. Two of them are *retractile*, meaning they can slide open or even be pulled ashore to let ships through.

- The life-size bronze elephant that stands in the United Nations Sculpture Garden on 46th Street was given to the UN in 1998 by the governments of Kenya, Namibia, and Nepal. But the anatomically correct animal sports a two-foot long…um…appendage. Today, plants strategically hide the controversial body part, but sadly, the garden is closed. You can still glimpse his front quarters from the street, though.

- Why are water towers and tanks so common on the rooftops of New York buildings? Because a water code from the 19th century specifies that all New York City buildings over six stories must have individual water storage enough to douse a fire above the sixth floor. Aqueducts and water pressure can take care of the first six floors; the amount of extra water and the size of the tank are commensurate with the number of extra floors.

- You can't fly directly to California from LaGuardia Airport. A perimeter rule set by the Port Authority limits the number of miles an airplane can fly nonstop out of LaGuardia. Maximum: 1,500. After Flushing Airport closed in 1984, most of its traffic was diverted to LaGuardia, so the Port Authority instituted the perimeter rule to avoid overcrowding. Two exceptions: 1) There is no cap on Saturday, and 2) the rule doesn't apply to flights to Denver (just over 1,700 miles) and some parts of the Caribbean—because nonstops from LaGuardia to those places were allowed before the rule was made.

*Above: The elephant sculpture "hides" in the United Nations Sculpture Garden.*
*Below: The Manhattan Bridge arch and colonnade has been designated a historic landmark.*

# Was There Ever an Orchard...

*Some things are pretty clear: Riverside Drive runs beside the river, Queens Boulevard extends through Queens...*

*A 17th-century map depicts New Amsterdam.*

## Big Apples

Once upon a time, there really was an orchard on Orchard Street, or at least where Orchard Street stands today. It was part of the vast farm belonging to James DeLancey, chief justice of the New York Supreme Court and a two-time lieutenant governor of New York State. In the 18th century, the DeLanceys were the largest single-family landholders in Manhattan, with an estate that extended from the Bowery to the East River and from Rivington Street to Division Street—an expanse that also included the tract that later became (surprise) Delancey Street.

## Going Dutch

There was once a wall on Wall Street too. The Dutch built it in 1653 to defend against attack by their archrivals in world domination, the British. The wall never was put to the test, though, and the Dutch eventually ceded New Amsterdam to the British in exchange for the South American colony of Suriname. After that, the British proceeded to anglicize the spelling and pronunciation of all the Dutch street names in Manhattan. Case in point: Broadway, which comes from the Dutch *breede weg*, or "wide street."

The Bowery also comes from a Dutch word—*bouwerij*, or farm. In the 17th century, Dutch governor Peter Stuyvesant had the largest one—around Third Avenue and Thirteenth Street, encompassing present-day Stuyvesant Street—and the route known as the Bowery ran from his farm to the city's business district.

## Water Everywhere

As the name implies, Water Street *is* pretty close to the East River—but not as close as it used to be. Originally, the street on the East River shoreline was Pearl Street, named for the tens of thousands of oyster shells found there. In the late 1600s, landfill was brought in to expand lower Manhattan, and with it came a new street—Water Street—which remained the waterfront until 1780, when more landfill created Front Street. In 1800 even more landfill led to the creation of South Street.

A few blocks away, Canal Street traces the path of a 40-foot-wide canal built in 1805 to drain the fetid water of Collect Pond (situated around Leonard Street between Lafayette and Centre, where Collect Pond Park now stands) into the Hudson River. Once that giant open sewer channel had done its job, it was filled in and Canal Street was built. Farther north, Spring Street was named for an underground spring discovered there when the

*Canal Street takes its name from a long-gone local waterway.*

# on Orchard Street?

*and the Grand Concourse still looks pretty grand. But how other city streets earned their names isn't as obvious.*

land belonged to Aaron Burr in the 1700s. And Minetta Lane comes from a Native American word that meant "devil's water."

## More about N Moore

No one paid much attention to N Moore Street (no period after the N) until the 1980s, when the "triangle below Canal"—TriBeCa—evolved from a collection of former manufacturing loft buildings into the trendy neighborhood of choice. You could argue that actor Robert DeNiro raised Tribeca's profile more than anyone; his production company is called Tribeca Productions, he's part owner of the Tribeca Grill restaurant, and he helped found the Tribeca Film Festival.

Once people took notice of N Moore, it was natural to wonder where the street's name came from. That's when the plausible explanation arose that N Moore Street was named for Nathaniel F. Moore, president of Columbia College from 1842 to 1849. Plausible, but a myth.

In reality, the street was named for Benjamin Moore, Nathaniel's uncle, who was also president of Columbia College (from 1801 to 1811), rector of Trinity Church, and the Episcopal bishop of New York. The N stands for North, to distinguish it from Moore Street in the Financial District. (That Moore Street was named for the place where ships were moored in the East River.)

## It Ain't Texas

Some out-of-towners like to claim that Houston Street is a tribute to Sam Houston, the Texas patriot for whom the city of Houston was named. But as any New Yorker knows, it's not pronounced "Hyew-ston"—it's "How-ston." William Houstoun, the true source of the street's name, was a delegate from Georgia to the Continental Congress from 1783 to 1786. (The Congress met in New York in 1785 and 1786.) In 1788 he married Mary Bayard, whose family's New York roots went back to the 1600s. Mary's father Nicholas Bayard constructed the street through his family's land and named it for his son-in-law. The route appeared on official maps as Houstoun Street until 1811, when the second "u" was dropped for reasons that remain unclear.

## Lost in New York

*In the 1992 film* Home Alone 2: Lost in New York, *young Kevin McCallister (Macaulay Culkin) gets lost in New York City and ends up staying at the Plaza Hotel (the only New York hotel he knows the name of). Here's some trivia about the movie.*

*Macaulay Culkin goofs off.*

- All shots inside the Plaza were filmed in an actual suite at the hotel, and the phone number given for the Plaza in the movie was one of the hotel's working numbers at the time.
- Real estate mogul Donald Trump makes a cameo: Kevin stops him in the Plaza's lobby to ask for directions. (Trump owned the hotel at the time.)
- The movie's director, Chris Columbus, also has a cameo: He walks by when Kevin goes into the toy store.
- Twelve-year-old Macaulay Culkin made $8 million for his work on this film, the largest salary ever paid to a child actor at that time.
- In the original film, Kevin visits many New York City landmarks, including the World Trade Center. But since the 2001 terrorist attacks, the scene at the World Trade Center has been removed from TV broadcasts.

# Strange Statues

*Instead of the Statue of Liberty, wouldn't you rather visit the Cement Sphinx?*

## Fallen Man

On March 12, 1888, Senator Roscoe Conkling was walking to the New York Club, a bar on 25th Street. It began to snow on the way, and the snow turned into a blizzard. Conkling collapsed and fell to the ground in Union Square. He never recovered and died a month later. His family asked the city to erect a Conkling statue in Union Square, but they were turned down—Conkling wasn't popular enough. But five years later, after repeated requests, a Conkling statue was built in Madison Square.

## White Angus

At the entrance to the Discovery Center, a hands-on children's museum in Binghamton, sits a 20-foot-tall fiberglass Black Angus bull named Blossom. But he isn't black. The giant animal is painted white and covered with orange, red, yellow, and purple flowers. (The imposing bull, who stands watch over the parking lot, started his career atop a steakhouse in the nearby town of Festal, until he moved to the Discovery Center in 2004.)

## To Climb or Not to Climb?

The official mascot of the Fontana Cement Company in Bayport, Long Island, is a 10-foot-tall goofy-faced replica of the ancient Egyptian Sphinx...made entirely of cement. It's been on Fontana's grounds since 1974.

Before that, it sat in front of the Anchorage Inn in Blue Point. Guests aren't allowed to climb on the Sphinx, but curiously, an inscription on it reads, "She who climbs to the Sphinx's head, a millionaire will surely wed."

*Blossom the bull resides at the Discovery Center.*

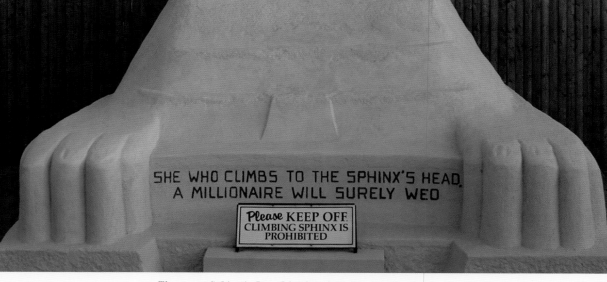

*The cement Sphinx in Long Island sends visitors mixed messages.*

# Off the Beaten Path

*New York has so many world-famous attractions that many lesser-known ones get overshadowed...like these.*

- **NEW YORK HALL OF SCIENCE**
**Location:** Queens
Located in Flushing Meadows–Corona Park, the Hall of Science opened in 1964 for the World's Fair. When the fair ended and the other exhibits closed, the Hall of Science stayed open. Today, it's the only hands-on science center in New York City and has more than 450 exhibits: You can peer into powerful microscopes and watch microbes move, figure out how much of your body weight is actually water, and play mini golf to learn that spaceships and golf balls are powered by the same forces.

- **PELHAM BAY PARK**
**Location:** The Bronx
At more than 2,700 acres, Pelham Bay Park is three times larger than Central Park and offers a much wilder experience. There's a wildlife sanctuary full of egrets, raccoons, blackbirds, and a salt marsh; Orchard Beach, the only public beach in the Bronx; and Split Rock, where 17th-century activist and reformer Anne Hutchinson supposedly hid before she was killed by a group of Native Americans fighting a war with the Dutch settlers.

- **ROOSEVELT ISLAND SKYTRAM**
**Location:** Manhattan
Instead of driving or taking a bus or the F train to visit Roosevelt Island, you can fly...sort of. The skytram takes about three minutes (and $2.25) to cross the East River from 59th Street/Second Avenue to Roosevelt Island, and from 250 feet above the ground, the views are spectacular. The tram made an appearance in the 2002 movie *Spider-Man*: The Green Goblin throws Mary Jane over the Queensboro Bridge at the same time that he drops a tram full of children, trying to force Spider-Man to choose between the woman he loves and the kids. (Spidey, of course, saves them all.)

*Right: The Mercury-Atlas D rocket towers over the New York Hall of Science Rocket Park.*

*Ralph Kramden's statue*

## The Statue of Ralph

In 1999 the TV Land cable channel paid tribute to Ralph Kramden of the 1950s series *The Honeymooners* by erecting an eight-foot statue of the fictional bus driver in Kramden's place of business: the New York–New Jersey Port Authority Bus Terminal in Manhattan.

# Where the Wild Things Are

*If you want to see exotic animals in their natural habitat, you could take a trip to Africa or Asia…or you could just catch a train to the Bronx.*

Above: A gorilla mom and baby cuddle at the Bronx Zoo.

## The Wild Bronx

With 265 acres and about 2 million visitors a year, the Bronx Zoo is the largest metropolitan zoo in the United States. It opened in 1899 and over the years has pioneered conservation techniques that benefit not only its 4,000 animal residents, but countless others across the globe. The Bronx Zoo was the first in the United States to let visitors donate to animal-conservation projects of their choice, and the first to house predators (lions) where they could see and smell their natural prey (antelope), which helped the animals keep their natural instincts sharp.

The zoo was also among the first to design enclosures that resembled natural habitats instead of cages. Because of the zoo's conservation efforts and dedication to building realistic habitats, it was also one of the first to display species rarely found in captivity. Here are just a few of the animal species that made a name for themselves at the Bronx Zoo.

## Congo Gorillas

One of the largest groups of western lowland gorillas in North America lives in New York. The Bronx Zoo's 6.5-acre Congo Gorilla

Forest, which opened in 1999, is the largest artificial African rain forest ever built and one of the most productive: It's the birthplace of at least six baby gorillas, the first of whom was Suki ("beloved" in Japanese) in 2000. Some gorillas that never produced offspring in other facilities are able to do so at Congo Gorilla Forest, presumably because the surroundings are so similar to their native Africa.

## Snow Leopards

In 1903 the Bronx Zoo was the first zoo in the Western Hemisphere to exhibit snow leopards, an exotic animal found in remote mountains of central Asia. Today, the animals live in the Himalayan Highlands exhibit, which includes trees, plants, caverns, and streams. Over 80 snow leopard cubs have been born at the zoo, more than at any other facility in the world. Bronx leopards have been sent to many other zoos, including the Central Park Zoo, which received three when it opened its snow leopard exhibit in 2009.

The Himalayan Highlands exhibit is also the site of important research. Snow leopards are notoriously elusive, making it difficult for scientists to study them in the wild. So in 2004, the World Wildlife Conservation used the exhibit to test ways to photograph snow leopards to count and identify them in the wild. Thanks to another study at the Bronx Zoo, cameras are now stationed in Asia.

*A snow leopard cub explores its Bronx Zoo exhibit.*

## Maleo Birds

Maleo birds are about the size of chickens and have bony faces and orange hooked beaks. They're also rare, endangered, and live only on the Indonesian island of Sulawesi… and at the Bronx Zoo. One reason they are so rare is their unusual nesting habits. A mother lays only one egg…and it's enormous, five times bigger than a chicken's. She buries it in warm sand or soil, and then takes off. When the chick hatches, it's on its own. Unlike other birds, newborn maleos can fly and defend themselves almost immediately. But the eggs are often attacked by wild dogs, pigs, and poachers, and their habitat is threatened by human development, so in 2006 there were fewer than 5,000 left

*Maleo birds thrive at the Bronx Zoo.*

in the world. The Bronx Zoo staff has been working with scientists in Sulawesi to restore the maleos' numbers. So far, they've helped the Indonesians hatch 4,000 maleo chicks successfully in the wild.

## Bison

In the early 19th century, an estimated 50 million bison roamed the plains of North America. But by 1900, only about 1,000 remained—they'd been nearly wiped out by overhunting and habitat destruction. So the Bronx Zoo established its own bison herd and, in 1907, sent 15 zoo-born bison by wagon and railroad to Oklahoma—the first time in American history that captive animals were purposely reintroduced into the wild. At the Wichita Mountains Wildlife Refuge, the Bronx bison helped to diversify the wild bison's gene pool, an important factor in revitalizing the species. Today, between 15,000 and 20,000 bison roam wild in North America.

# Hipster Spotting

*Of all the creatures native to New York, one of the most curious is the "hipster," found primarily in Brooklyn and Manhattan. Here's our guide to spotting one.*

If you answer "yes" to at least three of these questions, you have, in fact, found a hipster. Proceed with caution, don't mention that you use PCs, and keep quiet about your love of instant coffee.

- Does he have a mustache that was grown "ironically" because mustaches are out of date and uncool if grown to look cool?

- Does she have a favorite rock band? If you have heard of the band, this person is *not* a hipster.

- Is he rail-thin, and the only thing skinnier than him is the pair of skinny jeans he's wearing?

- Does she wear earmuffs, a fur cap, or a scarf when it's not winter?

- Does he have a job either in the arts or at an espresso bar?

- Is she perpetually staring at an iPhone, Macbook laptop, or iPad, which she uses to blog or post pictures of herself in fur caps on Tumblr?

- Do a disproportionate number of her sentences begin with the words, "This reminds me of something Malcolm Gladwell says"?

- Does she have bangs?

- Do her clothes look like they were purchased at Goodwill or a thrift store, but when you ask, you find out that her sweater cost $250?

- Does he say he lives not in New York or Brooklyn, but in a specific, tiny neighborhood?

- When you ask him what he watched on TV last night, does he respond, "I don't own a TV"?

- Does she participate in an adult league of a children's sport (such as kickball) or a retro sport (such as roller derby)?

*Hipster*

# Mind Your Manners

In the 1930s and '40s, New Yorkers were getting a reputation for being rude and messy, especially on the subway. They threw trash on the floor, put their feet up on seats where people wanted to sit down, and generally paid little attention to the needs of other passengers...or so said the MTA, which hired an artist named Amelia Opdyke "Oppy" Jones to create a series of posters reminding riders to be polite. What Jones came up with was a fake newspaper called the *Subway Sun*, whose "front page" (the face of the poster) included a quippy tip (like "Seats are for people, not packages") and an accompanying illustration (a well-dressed woman with shopping bags strewn about, as an elderly man searched for a place to sit down). Jones drew dozens of posters between 1935 and 1966. She also claimed to have coined the term "litterbug," which she said derived from "jitterbug." She first used it on a poster that stated, "Nobody loves a litterbug." Over the years, the *Subway Sun* posters also promoted fun places that New Yorkers could get to on the subway and advertised fare increases.

*A 1940s ad encourages riders to keep the subway clean.*

# Say What?

*More weird utterances from New York's politicians.*

"Freedom is about authority. Freedom is about the willingness of every single human being to cede to lawful authority a great deal of discretion about what you do."

**—Rudy Giuliani**

"I'm thinking about governing as the governor of this state, and that's what I'm going to do."

**—George Pataki**

"Not only is New York City the nation's melting pot, it is also the casserole, the chafing dish, and the charcoal grill."

**—John Lindsay**

"I've said that I'm not running [for president] and I'm having a great time being pres...being a first-term senator."

**—Hillary Clinton, 2004**

*Hillary Clinton*

*Former mayor Ed Koch in 2009*

"Life is indeed precious, and I believe the death penalty helps affirm this fact."

**—Ed Koch**

"And still the question, 'What shall be done with our ex-presidents?' is not laid at rest, and I sometimes think [journalist Henry] Watterson's solution of it, 'Take them out and shoot them,' is worthy of attention."

**—Grover Cleveland**

"Get action. Seize the moment. Man was never intended to become an oyster."

**—Theodore Roosevelt**

*This statue of Theodore Roosevelt, flanked by a Native American guide and an African American guide, greets visitors at the entrance of the American Museum of Natural History.*

# Wild Weather

*New Yorkers aren't strangers to extreme weather. But these storms tested the mettle of even the hardiest Empire State residents.*

*The New England Hurricane brought devastation to Long Island in 1938.*

## The Great White Hurricane

On March 11, 1888, a light rain began to fall in New York City. The temperature had been in the 50s for several days, unseasonably warm, and the forecast called for some cloudiness and then clearing skies. Forecasters couldn't have been more wrong: Over the next 24 hours, the temperature dropped more than 30 degrees, and 10 inches of snow fell. By March 13, the city was buried under more than three feet of snow.

And it wasn't just the city that got socked, either: Albany recorded four feet, and Saratoga Springs nearly five.

In New York City, the heavy snow knocked down power lines and telegraph cables throughout the boroughs. Drifts rose to the third stories of some houses—one man from Long Island told an incredible tale of snowshoeing to a nearby store on drifts that were 60 feet high. Some residents even claimed that the snow drifts were so high they didn't fully melt until July. In another legendary story, a man said he'd fallen into a snowdrift and hit his head on the hoof of a frozen horse. The gash on his temple was proof, he said, that he was the only man ever to be "kicked by a dead horse."

Transportation all along the eastern seaboard came to a standstill, stranding 15,000 people, and about 400 people died

*Residents of Albany slosh through the floodwaters in 1913.*

by the time the two-day storm was over. But New York and other eastern cities learned some valuable lessons: Many rebuilt their telegraph lines underground, started thinking about subways, and began using weather balloons to help make forecasting more accurate.

## The Great Flood

The winter of 1913 was warmer than usual all across the United States. In New York, Albany and Troy saw many January and February days with highs at least 10 degrees above normal...the upper 30s and 40s, even some 50s. That meant rain fell instead of snow. The result: clogged rivers.

By late March, the ground across the eastern United States was saturated, and much of Ohio and Pennsylvania had already

seen severe flooding. Then from March 23 to 27, rain fell nonstop across much of New York State. River towns from Olean to Albany found themselves under 10 feet of water. Power lines snapped, and rescuers faced the daunting challenge of reaching stranded people via boat because so many roads had washed away. In all the affected areas, more than 300 people died and nearly 65,000 were displaced.

## The New England Hurricane

In the fall of 1938, a junior meteorologist with the U.S. Weather Bureau (now the National Weather Service) tracked a storm out of the eastern Atlantic for more than a week and became sure it was headed for New England. But popular thinking at the time was that hurricanes "never" hit New England—the water in the northern Atlantic was supposedly too cold to sustain a tropical storm. So when the junior weatherman brought his concerns to his boss, he was told not to bother sending out an alert. Big mistake: The category 3 hurricane crashed into Long Island without warning at about 2:30 p.m. on September 21.

Forty-foot waves slammed into the south shore, winds roared at 120 mph with 180-mph gusts, and nearly 50 houses were immediately washed away. The storm moved fast; by late afternoon, it had blown into Connecticut and then on to Massachusetts. By the time it ended later that night, more than 700 people had died and 23,000 homes were destroyed or damaged. Clean-up estimates reached $300 million (more than $4 billion today).

# Opening Lines

*More great openings from great New York books.*

Dashiell Hammett

"I was leaning against the bar in a speakeasy on Fifty-Second Street, waiting for Nora to finish her Christmas shopping, when a girl got up from the table where she had been sitting with three other people and came over to me."

—**Dashiell Hammett,** *The Thin Man*

"Serene wasn't a word you could put to Brooklyn, New York. Especially in the summer of 1912. Somber, as a word, was better."

—**Betty Smith,** *A Tree Grows in Brooklyn*

"In those days, cheap apartments were almost impossible to find in Manhattan, so I had to move to Brooklyn."

—**William Styron,** *Sophie's Choice*

"Ok, don't panic. Don't panic. It's simply a question of being organized and staying calm and deciding what exactly I need to take. And then fitting it all in my suitcase."

—**Sophie Kinsella,** *Shopaholic Takes Manhattan*

# They Were Globetrotters?

*The high-energy and theatrical Harlem Globetrotters basketball team has been entertaining people since 1929, and over the years, they've employed dozens of big-name celebrities and sports stars as actual and honorary members. Here are five of the team's most surprising alumni.*

## 1. Pope John Paul II

The supreme pontiff of the Roman Catholic Church, Pope John Paul II, became an honorary Globetrotter on November 29, 2000, in a star-studded ceremony in St. Peter's Square in Vatican City. Members of the team commemorated the historic event by presenting His Holiness with an autographed basketball and a #75 jersey in honor of the team's 75th anniversary. It wasn't the first time the Globetrotters were granted an audience with a pope, though. The team also met Pope Pius XII in 1951 and 1952, Pope John XXIII in 1959 and 1963, and Pope Paul VI in 1968.

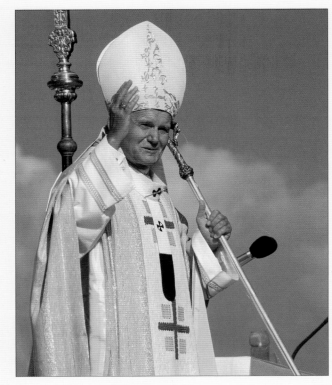

*Pope John Paul II was an honorary Globetrotter.*

## 2. Wilt Chamberlain

It might not seem like such a stretch that the 7' 1" NBA legend Chamberlain was once a Globetrotter, but he did it before becoming one of the world's most famous centers. A two-time All-American at the University of Kansas, "Wilt the Stilt" signed a one-year contract with the Globetrotters in 1958 (they paid him $50,000, a huge amount at the time). It was the only way he could play professional basketball—NBA rules prevented college juniors like Chamberlain from entering the league, but the Globetrotters were out of its jurisdiction. It proved to be money well spent, because his signing generated head-lines all across America and brought the team more fans (and ticket sales).

Chamberlain joined the NBA the following year, but he never forgot his time with the Globe-trotters, often calling it the most enjoyable part of his career. Chamberlain died in 1999, but was posthumously honored by the team in 2000, when the Globetrotters retired his jersey.

*Wilt Chamberlain became a Globetrotter when he was too young to play in the NBA.*

*Magic Johnson demonstrates his magic on the court.*

### 3. Bill Cosby

Cosby began his affiliation with the Globetrotters in December 1972, when he appeared in the debut episode of *The Harlem Globetrotters Popcorn Machine*, a short-lived variety show that aired on CBS. The team made the most of his appearance by signing the Emmy Award–winning comic to a lifetime contract—at $1 per year. (Cosby's rate was later increased to $1.05 in 1986 "to account for inflation.")

### 4. Magic Johnson

A 12-time NBA All-Star and a three-time NBA MVP, Earvin "Magic" Johnson first suited up for the Globetrotters in April 1997, during a college all-stars game. Johnson enjoyed the experience so much that he played for the team again in November 2003 in a game against his alma mater, Michigan State. Johnson tallied five points and four assists during the first 16 minutes of the 97–83 victory, helping the Globetrotters avenge a loss to MSU's Spartans in 2000 that had ended the team's 1,270-game winning streak (which had begun in 1995). Johnson is currently signed to a $1-a-year lifetime contract with the team and has a standing invitation to return at any time.

### 5. Bob Gibson

Although best known as an outstanding baseball player, Bob "Gibby" Gibson—then a talented athlete at Nebraska's Creighton University—helped a team of college all-stars defeat the Globetrotters in April 1957 in the World Series of Basketball, an annual three-week tournament. His performance was so impressive that the Globetrotters' owner, Abe Saperstein, signed Gibson to a one-year contract for the 1957–58 season…thereby delaying the start of his Major League Baseball career with the St. Louis Cardinals. Gibson so enjoyed the Globetrotters that he might have continued to play with them the next year if the Cardinals hadn't offered him a $3,700 bonus to join the team. Gibson went on to appear in nine All-Star Games and capture two World Series titles over his 17-year Hall of Fame career.

# The Narrowest House in New York...

…is located in Greenwich Village—it's only 8 feet, 7 inches wide and was once the home of poet Edna St. Vincent Millay.

*New York's narrowest house sold for $3.25 million in 2013.*

# There Goes the Neighborhood: Manhattan

*The island of Manhattan is home to dozens of neighborhoods with diverse histories. Here are the stories behind some of them.*

Times Square lights up at night.

- ***Manhattan*** comes from an Algonquin word, but nobody is sure what the original word was. Because of different Algonquin dialects and accents—plus hundreds of years of Europeans mispronouncing it—"Manhattan" could mean "island," "place for wood gathering"…or "place of general inebriation."

- **The Battery** was named for a battery (or grouping) of cannons placed at the southern tip of the island to defend the city in the 17th century.

- Not surprisingly, the **Flatiron District** is named for the iconic Flatiron Building, which took *its* name from the triangular plot of land on which it was built, shaped like a 19th-century iron.

- **Greenwich Village** was originally a small town north of the main settlement of New Amsterdam. The origin of the name "Greenwich" is disputed, however. Some historians think it was named after Greenwich, England, but others say that it's actually a corruption of a Dutch term, *Greenwijck* (or "Pine District"), which was the name of a now long-gone section of Long Island that was dotted with pine trees. In the 1670s, a wealthy landowner named Yellis Mandeville moved from

Greenwijck, Long Island, to the area that's now Greenwich Village, Manhattan, and many people believe he named his new neighborhood after the old one.

- No one's sure exactly where the term **Hell's Kitchen** came from, but during the 19th century, the west side of Manhattan was a notorious slum, with different areas sporting monikers like Battle Row or House of Blazes. Some historians suggest that "Hell's Kitchen" might have originally referred to a specific tenement; it also might have been borrowed from a similarly named slum in London. Despite the area's gentrification and the best efforts of real estate agents, the name has stuck.

- The term **SoHo** was coined in 1968, an abbreviation of "South of Houston Industrial Area." At the time, the neighborhood was becoming known for its artsy scene, and the sobriquet was inspired by the SoHo neighborhood in London, which stands for "South of

Holborn." It also spurred the creation of several other abbreviated place names in Manhattan: NoHo, "North of Houston"; NoLIta, "North of Little Italy"; and TriBeCa, "Triangle Below Canal."

- The **Tenderloin District** was a notorious red-light district in the 19th century, but its name doesn't have anything to do with prostitution. It actually refers to the quality of bribes a corrupt policeman could expect in this neighborhood. In 1876, when police inspector Alexander Williams (later nicknamed "Czar of the Tenderloin") began to oversee the area, he proclaimed, "I've been having chuck steak ever since I've been on the force, and now I'm going to have a bit of [better-quality] tenderloin." The name stuck.

- **Times Square** was known as Longacre Square until 1904, when the *New York Times* opened its headquarters there.

*Patrons enter the Tenderloin's famous dance hall, the Haymarket, in this 1907 painting.*

That year, Times Square hosted its very first New Year's Eve party. Fireworks were replaced by the iconic ball drop three years later.

- During the Revolutionary War, **Washington Heights** was home to Fort Washington, built on the highest point of Manhattan to defend it from the British. The fort gives both the neighborhood and the George Washington Bridge their names.

# The Inside Scoop on *30 Rock*

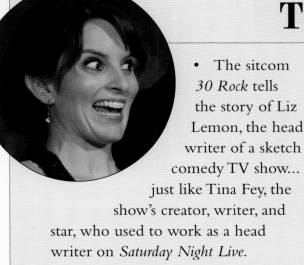

- The sitcom *30 Rock* tells the story of Liz Lemon, the head writer of a sketch comedy TV show... just like Tina Fey, the show's creator, writer, and star, who used to work as a head writer on *Saturday Night Live*.

- Although the show is set at 30 Rockefeller Plaza—the site of the *Saturday Night Live* studios—most of its interiors are filmed at Silvercup Studios in Queens.

- When she came up with the idea for the show, Tina Fey didn't intend to star in it herself. She changed her mind because NBC insisted that she take the part.

- Like Liz Lemon, Fey's first name is Elizabeth—Elizabeth Stamatina Fey. Her mother is Greek, and Stamatina is a traditional Greek name, meaning "one who stops."

- Fey's husband, Jeff Richmond, composes all the music for the show.

- In 2009 *30 Rock* received 22 Emmy nominations, the most for a comedy show in a single year.

# New York Q&A

*We have all kinds of questions about New York, so let's get started.*

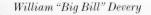

*William "Big Bill" Devery*

**Q. Where did all the brownstones come from?**
**A.** New York's brownstones—predominantly found in Brooklyn and on the Upper West Side—have become a city trademark, showing up in everything from *Sex and the City* to *Sesame Street*. This style of architecture prevailed in the late 19th and early 20th centuries, and the row houses were built for wealthy owners who didn't want to live in crowded apartments but still wanted to be close to the city. "Brownstone" refers to the building material—a brown sandstone with red and purple hues that was quarried mostly in Connecticut.

**Q. Which professional New York sports team was founded by two bartenders?**
**A.** What became the New York Yankees began in 1903 when city bartenders Frank Farrell and William "Big Bill" Devery bought the struggling Baltimore Orioles for $18,000, transplanted them to New York, and renamed them the Highlanders. That gave the city two teams: the National League's Giants and the American League's Highlanders, who lost their first game but made steady progress over the years. The team also started wearing pinstripes and took on the interlocking "NY" logo that was already being used as an honorary symbol for police officers killed in the line of duty. That logo has since become one of the most recognizable in sports… especially after 1913, when the Highlanders changed their name to the Yankees.

*Above: In a scene from* Sex and the City, *columnist Carrie Bradshaw works inside her New York brownstone (left).*

**Q. Are there any farms left in New York City?**

**A.** Yes, in Queens. The Queens County Farm Museum—a 47-acre patch of farmland in the Glen Oaks section—serves as the last tangible reminder of the agriculture that once characterized the borough. The farm has been operating since 1697, making it the oldest in New York State.

**Q. What was Rutherford Stuyvesant's claim to fame?**

**A.** Rutherford Stuyvesant was a descendant of the famous Peter Stuyvesant, the last head of the Dutch New Amsterdam colony and the namesake of Manhattan's Stuyvesant High School, the Bed-Stuy area of Brooklyn, and many other places. In 1869 Rutherford built the city's first luxury apartment building based on Parisian flats, which were common in France. Tenements for the poor had been around since the 1830s, but the idea of "good" families living in similarly close quarters brought out many critics who called the plan "Stuyvesant's folly." He pressed on, however, spending $100,000 on the five-story apartment building on 18th Street, between Irving Place and Third Avenue. There were 16 apartments on the first four floors, and a top floor with space for four artist studios. The apartments, which were the first in America to offer private bathrooms and

*The historic farmhouse at the Queens County Farm Museum*

running water, rented from $1,800 a year for a ground-floor apartment to around $1,000 for a fourth-floor suite. (Why cheaper at the top? No elevators.) Stuyvesant's building was occupied for 87 years and changed the way New Yorkers thought about apartments.

**Q. What's the oldest building in the Big Apple?**

**A.** New York City has a lot of old buildings, but a farmhouse built in 1652 takes this title. The Pieter Claesen Wyckoff Farmhouse (now Museum) in East Flatbush—as built by Pieter Claesen, a Dutch indentured servant who worked his way to freedom after arriving in New Amsterdam. (After the British took control of New Amsterdam and named it New York, Claesen adopted the more English-sounding last name Wyckoff.) The Dutch Colonial home that Claesen and his wife, Grietje Van Ness, built on Clarendon Road is now a National Historic Landmark.

*This statue of Peter Stuyvesant, patriarch of the famous New York family, was installed in Stuyvesant Square in 1941.*

# You Know You're a New Yorker When...

- Your front door has at least three locks (and possibly a snow shovel propped under the knob for extra protection).
- You'd climb three flights of subway stairs with crutches to avoid the subway elevator.
- You think of Central Park as "nature" and the Staten Island Ferry as a "romantic boat ride."

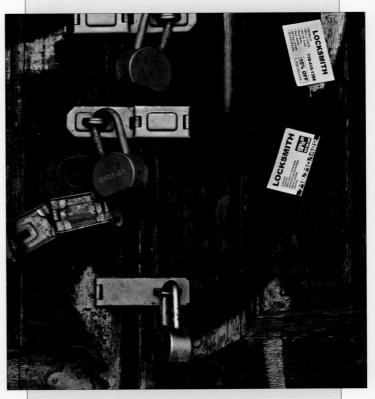
*Safety first! Many New Yorkers' front doors sport multiple locks.*

51

# NYC: Then and Now

*1964 was a big year: President Lyndon Johnson delivered his first State of the Union address, the Beatles made their live TV debut on the* Ed Sullivan Show, *and Jack Ruby was convicted of killing Lee Harvey Oswald. What was life like in New York City then, and how have things changed?*

**Then:** A subway token cost 15¢.
**Now:** Tokens have been replaced by Metrocards—the fare for a single ride is $2.75…and rising.

**Then:** A taxi ride from Midtown to LaGuardia Airport was about $4, not including tip or tolls. There was no partition between driver and passenger; you just reached over the front seat to hand your cash fare to the cabbie.
**Now:** It costs about $30 to take the same ride. That includes the starting fare (called the "drop") of $2.50—just for getting into the cab. It doesn't include the night surcharge of 50¢ between 8 p.m. and 6 a.m., a peak-hour weekday surcharge of $1 between 4 p.m. and 8 p.m., and a New York State surcharge of 50¢ per ride. And now there's a heavy-duty partition between passenger and driver, and you can pay your fare with a credit card.

**Then:** If you wanted info on traffic, school closings, or other official city happenings, you dialed (dialed!) 999-1234 and got a recorded announcement.
**Now:** Punch 311 into your cell (or go online) to navigate through dozens of options: Get the latest on traffic conditions and school closings, report a bad landlord, find a public beach, complain about a yellow cab, find out where to get a flu shot, carp about a New York City agency, or check up on just about anything else regarding the city.

**Then:** At Barbetta, a swanky restaurant on West 46th Street, a full dinner ran you about $12 per person.

*Barbetta has impressed diners for more than 100 years.*

**Now:** A full dinner at Barbetta costs upwards of $60 each.

**Then:** A double room at the Algonquin Hotel on West 44th Street cost between $14.50 and $20.50 per night. The rooms were small and cozy, with large closets and modern bathrooms.
**Now:** A double room at the Algonquin starts at $359.00. For this you get air conditioning, room service, bottled water, phones, high-speed Internet and WiFi, TV with remote, premium movie channels, radio, CD stereo, and an iPod dock.

**Then:** At National Bowling on Eighth Avenue (open 24/7) the charge per game was 50¢. Bowling shoes were free on weekdays before 4 p.m. and 20¢ a pair at other times.

*Taxi rides have gotten fancier—and pricier—since 1964.*

**Now:** At Bowlmor Lanes on West 44th Street in Manhattan (hours vary), the charge per person per game is $12.89. Shoe rental: $6.50…all the time.

**Then:** The White Horse Tavern on Hudson Street at West 11th was a bit of Britain in New York, and famous as the former hangout of hard-drinking Welsh poet Dylan Thomas. A Black-and-Tan, an ale, or a porter ran you 30¢. And sandwiches were about 50¢.

**Now:** Same tavern, same address, but a Black-and-Tan is about $6.50, an ale is $6.00, and sandwiches cost between $6.25 and $7.95.

**Then:** The Bronx Zoo charged 25¢ admission on Tuesdays, Wednesdays, and Thursdays; it was free the rest of the week and on holidays.

*The pricey Algonquin Hotel*

**Now:** "Total Experience" admission (including admission to the zoo and several rides and attractions) is $33.95 for adults, $23.95 for kids, and $28.95 for seniors.

**Then:** At Canine Styles on Lexington Avenue, your pooch got a basic grooming (including shampoo and pedicure) for $13 and up, depending on Fifi's size and the condition of her hair.

**Now:** At Biscuits & Bath on the Upper East Side, a full grooming includes bath, brushing, blowout, ear cleaning, and pedicure. And it costs about $85…for a small dog.

*An employee at Biscuits & Bath on the Upper East Side plays with the dogs in her care.*

# Talking about NYC

*How would you describe New York City?*

"New York is the biggest collection of villages in the world."

**—Alistair Cooke**

"I moved to New York City for my health. I'm paranoid, and it was the only place where my fears were justified."

**—Anita Weiss**

"Cut off as I am, it is inevitable that I should sometimes feel like a shadow walking in a shadowy world. When this happens I ask to be taken to New York City. Always I return home weary, but I have the comforting certainty that mankind is real and I myself am not a dream."

**—Helen Keller**

"When it's three o'clock in New York, it's still 1938 in London."

**—Bette Midler**

"The city is not a concrete jungle, it is a human zoo."

**—Desmond Morris**

"One belongs to New York instantly, one belongs to it as much in five minutes as in five years."

**—Thomas Wolfe**

"I miss New York. I still love how people talk to you on the street— just assault you and tell you what they think of your jacket."

**—Madonna**

*Alistair Cooke*

*Bette Midler*

*Madonna*

# City Cinema

*Lots of movies are set in New York, but they aren't all shot there. Here's a sampling of the ones that were.*

- *King Kong* (1933)
- *The Lost Weekend* (1945)
- *Kiss of Death* (1947)
- *Miracle on 34th Street* (1947 and 1994)
- *Cry of the City* (1948)
- *Sweet Smell of Success* (1957)
- *The Apartment* (1960)
- *Breakfast at Tiffany's* (1961)
- *Barefoot in the Park* (1967)
- *Midnight Cowboy* (1969)

- *The Panic in Needle Park* (1971)
- *Plaza Suite* (1971)
- *The French Connection* (1971)
- *The Godfather* (1972)
- *Serpico* (1973)
- *The Taking of Pelham 1 2 3* (1974 and 2009)
- *The Lords of Flatbush* (1974)
- *Dog Day Afternoon* (1975)
- *Taxi Driver* (1976)
- *Annie Hall* (1977)
- *Saturday Night Fever* (1977)
- *An Unmarried Woman* (1978)
- *All That Jazz* (1979)
- *Manhattan* (1979)
- *Fame* (1980 and 2009)

*The exterior shots of Breakfast at Tiffany's (1961) were filmed in New York.*

*John Travolta struts his stuff in Saturday Night Fever.*

*King Kong terrorizes New York in this 1933 poster.*

- *The Cotton Club* (1984)
- *Brighton Beach Memoirs* (1986)
- *Moonstruck* (1987)
- *Wall Street* (1987)
- *Coming to America* (1988)
- *Working Girl* (1988)
- *Do the Right Thing* (1989)
- *New York Stories* (1989)
- *When Harry Met Sally* (1989)
- *Goodfellas* (1990)
- *A Bronx Tale* (1993)
- *The Usual Suspects* (1995)
- *You've Got Mail* (1998)
- *Big Daddy* (1999)
- *Autumn in New York* (2000)
- *The Royal Tenenbaums* (2001)
- *Maid in Manhattan* (2002)
- *The Producers* (2005)
- *The Squid and the Whale* (2005)
- *Night at the Museum* (2006)
- *Inside Man* (2006)
- *Doubt* (2008)
- *Pride and Glory* (2008)
- *Sex and the City* (2008)
- *City Island* (2009)
- *The Extra Man* (2010)
- *The Adjustment Bureau* (2011)
- *The Avengers* (2012)
- *The Wolf of Wall Street* (2013)
- *The Secret Life of Walter Mitty* (2013)

*Captain America fights for freedom in a promotional still from* The Avengers.

# The Donald Speaks

- "As long as you're going to be thinking anyway, think big."

- "I could never have imagined that firing 67 people on national television would actually make me more popular, especially with the younger generation."

- "I try to learn from the past, but I plan for the future by focusing exclusively on the present. That's where the fun is."

- "Anyone who thinks my story is anywhere near over is sadly mistaken."

- "I wasn't satisfied just to earn a good living. I was looking to make a statement."

- "If you're interested in 'balancing' work and pleasure, stop trying to balance them. Instead make your work more pleasurable."

- "In the end, you're measured not by how much you undertake but by what you finally accomplish."

- "Money was never a big motivation for me, except as a way to keep score. The real excitement is playing the game."

- "Part of being a winner is knowing when enough is enough. Sometimes you have to give up the fight and walk away, and move on to something that's more productive."

- "It's tangible, it's solid, it's beautiful. It's artistic, from my standpoint, and I just love real estate."

- "Sometimes your best investments are the ones you don't make."

- "If you have to lie, cheat, and steal, you're just not doing it right. My career is a model of tough, fair dealing and fantastic success—without shortcuts."

- "The final key to the way I promote is bravado. I play to people's fantasies. People may not always think big themselves, but they can still get very excited by those who do. That's why a little hyperbole never hurts."

- "Everything in life is luck."

# Between the Lions

*Climb the steps between "Patience" and "Fortitude," and you'll find yourself in one of the most famous, important, and comprehensive libraries in the world.*

## A Tale of Two Libraries

In the late 19th century, New York was the second-largest city in the world (London was first), and many people realized that it would soon be a cultural capital, too. One of them was former New York governor Samuel J. Tilden, who left a $2.4 million trust to "establish and maintain a free library and reading room in the city of New York." The city already had two major libraries—the Astor and the Lenox—but both were research libraries, both were having financial difficulties, and only the Astor was open to the public. Seeing an opportunity, Tilden's trustees came up with a plan to combine the Astor and Lenox Libraries and the Tilden Trust to form what would become the New York Public Library (NYPL, or "nipple" to devoted users). The plan was finalized on May 23, 1895, and John Shaw Billings, an eminent librarian and surgeon, became the new director.

## House of Books

Billings was a visionary, too—he wanted a spectacular building that could house the riches of the Astor and Lenox Libraries, while offering comfortable facilities for scholars and ordinary readers alike. The chosen site was the former Croton Reservoir, a two-block area on Fifth Avenue between 40th and 42nd Streets that had once held most of the freshwater used in the city. The new library would have seven floors, a huge reading room, and 30,000 reference books. It would also have the world's fastest book-to-user delivery system: A patron would send a call slip to the "closed stacks," or storage rooms, downstairs via a pneumatic tube, and in a matter of minutes, the book would be sent up to the reading room via dumbwaiters. For two years, 500 workers dismantled the old reservoir and prepared the site. Construction finally began in May 1902, and the official dedication took place on May 23, 1911.

Total cost: $9 million. On May 24, when the library first opened its doors, more than 30,000 New Yorkers rushed in.

## NYPL Facts and Figures

Over the years, NYPL has racked up an impressive list of stats. Here are some of the most important.

- In-person visits per year: 18 million
- Online visits per year: 24 million
- Only boroughs not included in the NYPL system: Brooklyn and Queens. (They have their own independent library systems.)
- Total items in the branch and research libraries: 51.6 million
- Items in the Photography Collection: 500,000
- Items in the Map Division: 433,000 sheet maps, and 20,000 books and atlases published between the 15th and 21st centuries
- Historic menus: 26,000
- Historic U.S. postcards: more than 100,000
- Categories the online and phone reference system ASK NYPL will not answer questions about: crosswords or contests, children's homework, and philosophical speculation

## Gimme Shelter

Anyone who has visited a branch library on a sweltering day (or a frigid one) knows that the NYPL is a haven. Libraries, as former head of NYPL Paul LeClerc said in 2008, "are the only indoor communal spaces left in New York." People with no air conditioning cool off there; homeless men and women warm up. But there are rules. Anyone who visits a NYPL branch is expected to adhere to the following:

- You may not wash your clothes or bathe in the restrooms.
- No loud talking on your cell phone.
- Don't bring knives, guns, or any other weapons to the library.
- No obscene gestures, abusive language, or lewd behavior.
- No shopping carts, bicycles, or scooters.
- No napping in the library or sleeping in the entryway.
- No dropping your kid at the library and forgetting to pick her up.
- No hacking or using the Internet for any illegal activity.
- You must wear clothes and shoes, and you can't smell bad.

# New York's "X Files"?

When it comes to rumors of strange happenings, the old military base at Camp Hero—at the eastern tip of Long Island—may have some of the weirdest. Established in 1942 during World War II to protect against the very real threat of a German submarine attack on the United States, the base closed after the war...or so says the U.S. military. Conspiracy theorists tell a different tale. According to them, soldiers at Camp Hero worked on an experiment during World War II, in which the U.S. Navy teleported a destroyer, the USS *Eldridge,* from Pennsylvania to Virginia and back again. Supposedly the ship transported successfully, but the sailors on board suffered a terrible fate: Some became fused to the ship during the teleportation. Others went insane after seeing what had happened to their shipmates. After the war, say the conspiracy buffs, Camp Hero expanded into a vast underground city of tunnels and research labs where scientists studied time travel, teleportation, aliens, mind control, and hyperspace wormholes.

The State of New York isn't buying it (and neither are we). Officially, Camp Hero is just a park—415 acres of trails and greenery open to the public 365 days a year. There are still some abandoned military buildings on the grounds, and the park service hopes to eventually convert some of them into a museum telling the story of Camp Hero's role in World War II. Whether the museum will include teleportation devices or reconstructions of alien spaceships remains to be seen.

*A bunker at Camp Hero leads underground.*

# There Goes the Neighborhood: Staten Island

*Before Staten Island became known for its landfill, it was known for its trees. (Yes...really.)*

*A vintage ad extols the beauty of St. George, Staten Island.*

- The Lenape Indians who originally lived in the area that's now **Staten Island** called it *Monacnong* ("Enchanted Woods"). And in 1776, a British soldier referred to the future borough as the "paradise of the world" because its forests were so beautiful. But the Dutch who settled there in the 1600s had already called it *Staaten Eylandt*, after the name of the Dutch parliament (the Staaten-Generaal). And that's the name that stuck.

- In 1872 the American Linoleum Manufacturing Company moved into Travisville and changed the community's name to Linoleumville. ("Travis" was the last name of a man who owned a lot of land in the area.) By the time the factory closed in 1931, residents were tired of—and embarrassed by—their town's name, so they voted on another name change—to **Travis**. Only four people (out of more than 300) voted to keep Linoleumville.

- The neighborhood of **Bulls Head** gets its name from the Bull's Head Tavern that stood at the intersection of Richmond Avenue and Victory Boulevard. During the Revolutionary War, British supporters used the tavern as a base of operations.

- **Arthur Kill** is the name of the tidal strait that separates Staten Island from New Jersey. It comes from a Dutch term, *achter kill*, which means "back channel," because the waterway is essentially "behind" Staten Island. (*Kille* is Dutch for "water channel" or "riverbed.") When the English moved into the area, they kept the term but anglicized the spelling.

*Facing page, top: The Bayonne Bridge connects Staten Island to New Jersey.*

*The Staten Island ferry terminal beckons travelers.*

# Dunkin' Doughnuts

There's no way to know for sure who was the first person to dunk a doughnut into a cup of coffee, but we do know who made it popular. In the 1920s, silent film star Mae Murray—best known for her full, pouty lips—accidentally dropped a piece of her doughnut into a cup of coffee while eating at a New York deli. Her friends were aghast, waiting to see what she'd do, but Murray just fished out the doughnut, popped it into her mouth, and declared it "delicious." Word of Murray's unusual eating habit spread to Hollywood, and suddenly doughnut-dunking appeared in movies like *Duck Soup* (with Groucho Marx) and *It Happened One Night* (with Clark Gable and Claudette Colbert). Thanks, Mae!

*Clark Gable and Claudette Colbert ponder how to dunk a doughnut in* It Happened One Night *(1934).*

# Shop Till You Drop

*Once upon a time, no self-respecting New York lady went shopping without donning white gloves, a fancy chapeau, and her nicest dress...while the stores duked it out for her money.*

## In the Beginning

In 1856 an Irish immigrant named Alexander Turney (A.T.) Stewart opened the first department store in New York City...A.T. Stewart at 280 Broadway. Inside the building—nicknamed the "Marble Palace" because of a showy exterior that featured expensive marble and Italian architecture—shoppers could find all kinds of European goods at decent prices. Best of all, everything was in one place, so they didn't have to run around town to dozens of shops.

Within a few years, A.T. Stewart was joined by several new department stores, and the section of Broadway between Eighth and 23rd Streets became known as "Ladies' Mile" because so many of the stores catered to women. Shopping on the Ladies' Mile was a fantastic and fancy affair: Stores lured women with marble floors, personal shoppers, and high tea on mezzanines overlooking the stores.

## And Stewart Begat...

The owners of the stores on the Ladies' Mile soon realized, though, that uptown was where the money was. The city's most fashionable families lived closer to Central Park, so New York's high-class shopping hub gradually shifted north, until it centered around Fifth Avenue between Midtown and the park. The quintessentially New York department stores that lined the streets helped make Fifth Avenue (and Park, Melrose,

*The A. T. Stewart building sits at 280 Broadway.*

and Lexington to the east) some of the "most expensive streets in the world":

- **Lord & Taylor** was the first store on Fifth Avenue to install an elevator and the first to set up grand Christmas displays in its windows each holiday season. Technically, this store opened before A.T. Stewart, but it sold only a handful of specialized things: mostly clothing and lingerie in the 1820s. What became Lord & Taylor wasn't technically a "department store" until 1861, when it varied its merchandise. To this day, the Fifth Avenue store starts each morning with the national anthem.

- Opened in 1892, **Abercrombie & Fitch** originally catered to men by selling mostly hunting, fishing, and outdoor gear. Before the company sold its brand in the 1980s and the new owners switched over to casual wear for men and women, the store outfitted such adventurous celebrities as Teddy Roosevelt, Ernest Hemingway, and Howard Hughes. Abercrombie & Fitch's original Manhattan store (which closed in 1977) even had a shooting range in the basement.

- **Bloomingdale's** opened in 1872 on the Lower East Side but moved uptown in 1886. By the 1920s, the store covered an entire city block at 59th and Lexington. Bloomie's execs mastered the use of direct-mail catalogs, and the store marketed itself as being "fashion-forward" with its avant-garde designer clothing. In 1961 Bloomie's also became the first department store to design its own shopping bags.

- The first **Saks** store opened in 1902 on Ladies' Mile as Saks and Company. In 1923 Saks merged with Gimbel Brothers Inc. (but kept the name of Saks). Finally, in 1924, Saks Fifth Avenue—founded by Horace Saks and Bernard Gimbel—opened on Fifth Avenue near St. Patrick's Cathedral. Merging the two huge department store families (the Saks and the Gimbels) was supposed to create a megastore that had a reputation for

offering only the most lavish and up-scale merchandise. It worked.

- The first **Macy's** store—a small Sixth Avenue emporium that sold dry goods—opened in 1858. The first day, it netted $11 in sales; the second was a little better…$51 worth of merchandise was sold. But thanks to savvy merchandising and good business sense, Macy's sold almost $100,000 by the end of the next year—an amazing amount for the times—and things just got better from there. Within four years of opening, Macy's was a New York City destination, particularly at Christmas. It was the first New York department store to invite Santa in for annual visits, and in 1867, it was the first store to stay open until midnight on Christmas Eve.

*Jackie Kennedy Onassis shops at Bonwit's in 1970.*

In 1902 Macy's opened a much larger store on 34th Street near Herald Square. It boasted 33 elevators, four escalators, and that cool pneumatic tube system that sent payments to clerks in an upstairs office. The building eventually grew to 11 stories of retail heaven.

## Gone, but Not Forgotten

Not every fancy department store that opened in New York City managed to stick around. These three fought the good fight but lost:

- Opened in 1895, **Bonwit's** (originally Bonwit Teller) was known for high-end merchandise and the higher-than-average salaries paid to its upper-management employees. Located on Fifth Avenue, the

*Bloomingdale's has been a shopper's haven for more than a century.*

store merged and morphed over the years until its parent company went bankrupt in 1989. But in the store's heyday, Marilyn Monroe, Audrey Hepburn, and Jacqueline Kennedy Onassis all shopped there.

- **Altman's** (also known as B. Altman's) opened in 1865 and became Fifth Avenue's first large-scale department store in 1906. Altman's was famous for its lavish Christmas window displays and its in-house restaurant, which was built to look like Scarlett O'Hara's house in *Gone With the Wind*. In 1989 the

corporation filed for bankruptcy; it closed the next year.

- Not originally a New York store (the first ones opened in Indiana, Wisconsin, and Pennsylvania), **Gimbels** opened in 1910 near Macy's in Herald Square. The first Manhattan store to sport a bargain basement, Gimbels boasted that they would not be undersold. Giant enough to be considered the main competitor of Macy's for many years, Gimbels bought out Saks and Company in the 1920s. But by 1987, Gimbels was no longer making enough to stay afloat and had to close its doors.

*Altman's held this Fifth Avenue location until it closed in 1990.*

# Hey, Taxi!

*If you've ever hailed a cab after a game at Madison Square Garden, you know it takes some insider knowledge. Here are a few facts and trivia about those New York cabs.*

- The first metered taxis showed up on New York City streets in 1907, the brainchild of Harry N. Allen, a New Yorker who was angry that a hansom cab driver charged a friend $5 (about $113 today) for a 0.75-mile trip.

- Allen's first taxis were red and French-made; he introduced 65 of them to Manhattan on October 1. A year later, he had a fleet of 700.

- The first taxi strike took place in October 1908, when 500 drivers at Allen's New York Taxicab Company walked out because they wanted to be considered full-time employees and they wanted Allen to supply free gas. (Rising gas prices were making

them lose money, they said.) But Allen wanted to keep in place the system he'd set up: Cabbies rented their uniforms, cabs, etc. from him and used the money from their fares to pay for it all. After a violent month of protests, the strikers gave in. A similar system still exists today.

- Businessman John Hertz founded the Yellow Cab Company in 1915. He was the first to paint taxis yellow. Why? He thought it was the easiest color for the eye to see. (Hertz also went on to found Hertz Rent-a-Car.) In 1967 New York City mandated that all of its taxis had to be yellow so they would be easy to spot at a distance.

- New York City's most famous taxi model was the Checker cab, which first appeared in 1922 and had its heyday in the 1930s and '40s. Checker cabs became iconic to the city, but most of them were actually manufactured in Michigan.

- The first woman to drive a New York City taxi began work in 1925; in the 1960s, about 10 percent of all cab drivers were women. By 2008 that number had dropped to 1 percent.

- There are more than 12,000 licensed cabs in New York City…50,000 if you also include limousines and other types of hired cars.

# Celebrity 101

*Get to know your New York celebrities.*

*Lucille Ball and her husband, Desi Arnaz, attend a 1953 news conference about her short association with the Communist Party.*

- CNN anchor **Anderson Cooper** was once a child model. At 10 years old, he had a contract with the Ford Modeling Agency.

- In 2004 **Jennifer Lopez's** mother, Guadalupe (a Westchester County teacher), won $2.4 million at an Atlantic City casino.

- Before becoming an Academy Award–winning actor, **Adrien Brody** did magic shows at children's birthday parties. His stage name: the Amazing Adrien.

- **Humphrey Bogart's** mother, Maud, worked for many years as a commercial artist and illustrator, and around 1900, she submitted a drawing of her infant son to Mellin's Baby Food. The company's execs liked the little boy's chubby cheeks and put him in all of their ad campaigns. Bogey said later, "There was a period in American history when you couldn't pick up a goddamned magazine without seeing my kisser on it."

- As a kid, **Tom Cruise** wanted to be a priest. He even enrolled in a seminary, but dropped out after a year.

- **Robert De Niro** and **Martin Scorsese** grew up within just a few blocks of each other in Manhattan's Little Italy in the 1950s, but they didn't actually meet until 1972, when they were introduced at a party.

- **Taye Diggs's** real first name is Scott. "Taye" comes from his childhood nickname, "Scottaye."

- **Rosie O'Donnell's** senior classmates at Commack High School on Long Island voted her "Most Popular."

- In 1936, as a favor to her grandfather, **Lucille Ball** joined the Communist Party. Fast-forward to the 1950s: When the House Un-American Activities Committee began investigating entertainers with Communist ties, Ball appeared on their list. But ultimately, the committee decided that she wasn't a Communist after all (she'd never contributed any money or attended any meetings) and dropped the investigation.

*Tom Cruise in* Risky Business, *the movie that made him a star.*

# When You Gotta Go...

*There are some spots in New York that you might like to visit, but you wouldn't want to live there because...well...nobody actually "lives" there.*

## The African Burial Ground

**Where:** At the corner of Duane and Elk streets, lower Manhattan

**The story:** In 1991, workmen constructing a new office building dug 20 feet below the surface and discovered a nearly six-acre, 300-year-old burial ground for African slaves and freedmen. In the 1600s, New York City was the largest port for slave trading in the American colonies. In fact, the very first sales tax in New Amsterdam (later New York) was levied on "human cargo," and in 1709 the British set up a slave market on Wall Street. At the time, the local government made little distinction between free and enslaved Africans (all were referred to as "slaves") and refused to bury Africans in cemeteries alongside whites. So the city set up a separate African burial ground about a mile outside of what was then the city limits.

The U.S. government outlawed new slave importation in 1807, and by then, New York's African burial ground had filled in with debris and was developed. By the time slavery ended for good in 1865, the burial ground was largely forgotten—until that day in 1991. In all, an estimated 10,000 people were buried at the site, including 21 men executed after a slave rebellion in 1712. After the burial ground's discovery, work on the office building was halted to allow for a proper excavation, and the building was redesigned to accommodate a memorial at the site. In 2006 President George W. Bush declared the burial ground a national monument, and a visitor's center (located at 290 Broadway) opened in 2010.

## Hartsdale Pet Cemetery

**Where:** Westchester County

**The story:** It's fitting that a veterinarian founded the largest pet cemetery in the world. Dr. Samuel Johnson was a veterinary surgeon in New York City and the state's

*Forensic sculptor Frank Bender re-created three people for this statue based on their remains found in the African Burial Ground.*

*A dog statue "guards" the rear entrance of the Hartsdale Pet Cemetery.*

first official veterinarian. In 1896 a distraught pet owner visited him with a delicate problem—where to bury her beloved, but recently deceased, dog. Johnson volunteered a spot on his Westchester property, in his apple orchard.

Not long afterward, Johnson told the story to a friend, who was a reporter. Within a few days, the story was in print… and Johnson was inundated with requests from bereaved pet owners. He couldn't turn them away, so the apple orchard became a cemetery. In 1914 Johnson officially formed what he called the Hartsdale Canine Cemetery, though it was open to animals of all kinds.

Today more than 70,000 animals are interred there…along with about 700 people who wanted to be buried with their pets. "Residents" include rabbits, birds, Westminster Kennel Club ribbon-winners, dogs belonging to Diana Ross and Elizabeth Arden, a lion cub, monkeys, and many everyday—but no less special—animals.

Some of the epitaphs at Hartsdale:

- "For You I Wait, At Heaven's Gate"
- "Our Beloved Pudgy"
- "Thor: Good Boy"
- "My dear little true-loving hearts, who would lick the hand that had no food to offer."

## The New York City Cemetery (Potter's Field)

**Where:** Hart Island, western edge of Long Island Sound, the Bronx
**The story:** Over the years, New York City has had several potter's fields cemeteries where people are buried when they can't afford a private funeral. Bryant Park, Madison Square Park, and Washington Square Park all started as potter's fields. But today, the most famous one is located on Hart Island, a 101-acre stretch of land in Long Island Sound.

Hart Island got its start in New York history as a Civil War prison camp for Confederate soldiers. It also housed an isolation area for yellow fever patients, a charity hospital, an insane asylum, a boys' workhouse, a missile base, and disciplinary barracks for wayward servicemen during World War II. Through its many incarnations, the island was often used by the city as a burial ground, but it didn't become New York's official indigent cemetery until 1991.

Today, the New York Department of Corrections operates the Hart Island potter's field, and inmates from Riker's Island perform the burials as part of their work details. (Each prisoner is paid about 50¢ an hour.) Coffins are placed in large, common burial plots, and the location of each one is recorded. More than 850,000 bodies rest there today, making Hart Island the largest public (i.e., tax-funded) cemetery in the world. Hart Island isn't open to the public, but family members can usually get permission to visit their relatives' graves.

# Lost and Found

In 2008 people in the five boroughs left about 19,000 items on New York City's subways and buses—42 percent of those things were returned to their owners. Unsurprisingly, some of the most frequently lost (and found) items include IDs, cell phones, iPods, wallets, keys, shoes, and toys. But on the informational posters the MTA puts up in the city's buses and subway cars, the pictures of "suggested" lost items include a crutch, a set of false teeth, a computer mouse, and a cobra. And maybe those possibilities aren't so far-fetched: According to the *New York Post*, in 2008 the MTA found (among other things) "a fake limb, a used cooking pot, and a trumpet."

# Scoop the Poop

*In the early 1970s, dog poop had reached critical mass on the sidewalks of New York City—an estimated 125–250 tons were deposited per day. Some citizens were sick of it and the Department of Sanitation couldn't cope. It was time for action.*

*Abe Beame*

## Lords of Dogtown

New York has always been a doggie town, but for many years, dog owners were accustomed to letting their dogs do their business and walking away, leaving the poop on the sidewalks for other people to step in and around. There was a long-standing city ordinance against letting dogs poop on public property, but dog owners generally ignored it. As far back as the 1930s, the Department of Sanitation—trying to take a practical approach—began posting "Please Curb Your Dog" signs, meaning that dogs should be made to poop in the gutters. A few dog owners complied; most protested that it was unsafe to make their dogs go in the street, where they might be hit by cars. So the poop problem got worse with each passing decade. Since New York City didn't have the manpower to police the delinquent dog owners, there was no real incentive to obey the law.

## Lenient Lindsay

By the early 1970s, the city's level of dog-poop tolerance had changed, and the filthy sidewalks and parks sparked tempers everywhere. Mayor John Lindsay recognized the poop problem but refused to address it… except to express his opinion that dogs should relieve themselves in their owners' apartments, not on the streets.

But complaints about the dog droppings and the law-breaking dog owners were flooding the city's Environmental Protection Administration (EPA) and the City Council. Something had to be done. On May 16, 1972, EPA official Jerome Kretchmer proposed a new ordinance: People would have to pick up their dogs' droppings, or pay a $25 fine. Dog owners were convinced that this was just the first step down a slippery slope that would end with dogs being banned from nearly everywhere in the Big Apple. Local politicians were caught in the middle—they were afraid to support the law because they'd been warned that they wouldn't be reelected if they did, but they were also tired of hearing the dog-doo complaints from environmental groups, civic groups, block associations, and private citizens. Kretchmer viewed his proposal as a simple compromise: Pet owners could keep their dogs, but the poop would cease to be a problem. The ordinance didn't pass.

## Beame's B-List

The next mayor, Abe Beame, inherited the poop problem from Lindsay, but by the time he was elected in 1974, the city was mired in a financial recession and the new mayor didn't consider dog poop to be an A-list issue. In fact, the city's EPA was downsized almost out of existence in 1977. But complaints about dog poop kept coming. Beame's wife Mary tried to lead an antipoop campaign—complete with posters reading "Parks are for recreation, not defecation"—but it didn't have much impact on a city teetering on the edge of bankruptcy. Sanitation Commissioner Anthony Vaccarello proposed another impractical solution: a city tax on dog food. If dog food were more expensive, he reasoned, owners would feed their dogs less food: less food in, less poop out. That law also failed to pass.

## Koch's Cleanup

It fell to Mayor Ed Koch, elected in 1978, to cope. Unable to get action from a City Council afraid to go head-to-head with dog owners, Koch went straight to the state government in Albany, where he presented the canine waste problem as a statewide issue. But in order to circumvent the New York City Council and override "home rule" (a constitutional issue), the state legislature had to make the proposed pooper-scooper law apply to more cities than just New York.

So State Senator Franz Leichter and State Assemblyman Edward H. Lehner cowrote the Canine Waste Law, which called for the "removal of canine wastes in cities with a population of 400,000 or more persons." Dog owners who failed to pick up their dogs' poop would be fined $100. In June 1978, the law passed by a narrow margin. Aside from New York City, only Buffalo met the population criterion, so New York was now the first major American city to have such a law.

## Enforcement Blues

Enforcing the law was going to be just as hard as passing it had been, but since it wouldn't go into effect for a full year, Mayor Koch had time to get people used to the idea.

These days, New York sidewalks are significantly cleaner and the fine has been raised to $250. But that doesn't mean the problem has been solved completely. In 2009 there were 4,443 dog-poop calls to the city's complaint line—the highest number in three years. So the saga continues.

*Antipoop signs encourage cleanliness in New York.*

67

# There Goes the Neighborhood: Brooklyn

*Nearly 15 percent of all Americans can trace their family history back to Brooklyn, one of the most ethnically diverse areas of the country. Here are just a few of the histories of some of the borough's neighborhoods.*

*Diners line up outside a Grimaldi's in DUMBO.*

- ***Brooklyn*** comes from the town Breukelen, in the Netherlands. When the Dutch settled New Amsterdam, they gave the name to a small village near what's now Brooklyn Heights. When the Dutch lost New Amsterdam to the British in the 1660s, the new colonizers kept the name and the pronunciation, but changed the spelling.

- **DUMBO** is an acronym for Down Under the Manhattan Bridge Overpass, and even though the name is relatively new (the area has only been called DUMBO since the late 1970s), there's already debate about how it started. Some people say that David Walentas, a New York developer, coined the term—as he was buying up properties in the area, he wanted a cool-sounding acronym for the new neighborhood... like SoHo in Manhattan. Others say that residents actually started calling the area DUMBO to discourage gentrification (a silly sounding neighborhood was more likely to put off trendy residents). Either way, DUMBO stuck. Before that, the area was known as Rapailie, Olympia, Fulton Landing, and Gairville.

- The Dutch originally called **Red Hook** "Roode Hoek": *roode* for the red clay soil, and *hoek*, "point," because part of it "points" into the East River.

- **Flatbush** also comes from two Dutch words: *vlacke*, or "flat," and *bosch*, "woodland." East Flatbush, though, had a more colorful name—during the 1800s, it was called Pigtown, because it was full of shanties and pig farms.

- Around 1670, farmers in Flatbush started moving out of town in search of open land. Many of them settled in an area near Jamaica Bay, called the "east woods." But as more people moved in, the area became a small town in its own right... **New Lots**, for all the new parcels of land those farmers had settled.

- **Weeksville** gets its name from a former slave named James Weeks, who bought some land on the outer edges of Brooklyn in 1838 and created a self-sufficient community for free, professional African Americans. (New York City's first black police officer, Wiley Overton, lived in Weeksville, and the city published the *Freedman's Torchlight*, one of the first black newspapers in the United States.) By the mid–20th century, though, the town had been absorbed into Crown Heights and mostly forgotten. That is, until a historian named James Hurley rediscovered the town, which led to an archaeological dig to unearth important artifacts. Many of the buildings were later added to the National Register of Historic Places.

- When the Dutch first visited the area that became **Coney Island**, there were rabbits everywhere...so many that the settlers named the peninsula *Konijn Eiland* (Rabbit Island). When the British took over, they anglicized the spelling, as usual.

- Before the 1920s, the water in **Sheepshead Bay** teemed with marine life, in particular a flatfish with stubby teeth called the *sheepshead*. But as developers moved in and started building houses along the water and polluting the bay, the sheepsheads and many other marine animals left or died off.

*The amusement park at Coney Island features the famous Wonder Wheel.*

# In the Big House

*In most of New York's prisons, inmates are known for the single worst crime they've committed…or been caught for. But a few prisoners also made names for themselves for what they did while they were doing time.*

*Lil Wayne released this album while in prison.*

**Inmate:** Lil Wayne, Grammy winner and self-proclaimed "Best Rapper Alive"
**Locked up in**: Rikers Island
**While in prison:** In 2010 Lil Wayne released the album titled *I Am Not a Human Being* (which shot to #1 on the Billboard charts), collaborated on a song with rappers Drake and Jay-Z, was sued by a record producer, and posted regular blog entries. The last month of his incarceration was spent in solitary confinement because he was caught with contraband—not drugs or weapons, but an iPod charger and earphones.

**Inmate:** John Colt, brother of revolver inventor Samuel Colt
**Locked up in:** The Tombs
**While in prison:** The day before Colt's execution in 1842, he married his housekeeper. Hours later, he committed suicide in his cell by stabbing himself through the heart. At the same time, a candle (or lamp) ignited a fire that swept through the prison and destroyed part of the roof. Several prisoners escaped, and Colt's bride was never seen again, sparking a rumor that she set the fire while Colt faked his death, substituted another body for his own, and escaped.

*A postcard shows the Tombs prison, built in 1902.*

*The prison on Rikers Island has housed some of New York's most notorious criminals.*

*An 1874 drawing shows John Colt's wedding in the Tombs.*

**Inmate:** Drifter Eddie White
**Locked up in:** Rikers Island
**While in prison:** By 1994 White had broken out of Rikers Island three times. (He'd been locked up for the murders of two people and sentenced to 200 years to life.) The breakouts earned him the respect of inmates, who dubbed him "Rabbit Man" for his quickness. In one escape, he allegedly killed two more people, but those charges were dismissed when the judge noted that he was already going to die in jail.

**Inmate:** Robber Ronald Tackman
**Locked up in:** Rikers Island
**While in prison:** In October 2009, Tackman donned a suit for his trial and walked out of prison by posing as a lawyer—he asked, "Which way is out?" and a guard escorted him. (Two days later, he was reapprehended.) That con worked because Tackman was a crafty master of

*Ronald Tackman after his recapture*

disguise. During stickups, he wore a fake nose or a big-rimmed gangster hat. And in jail, Tackman once took over a prison van using a "weapon" carved out of soap.

**Inmate:** Con artist Tuvia Stern
**Locked up in:** The Tombs
**While in prison:** In June 2009, Stern threw a lavish bar mitzvah for his son… behind bars. Held in the prison gym, the gala had 60 guests, a band, and catered kosher food. Attendees were even allowed to keep their cell phones, a big no-no in prison, and the jail paid officers overtime for the event. Four months later, Stern threw another party, this time for his daughter's engagement. When the city's corrections commissioner found out about the parties, he suspended the prison rabbi who'd overseen the bar mitzvah and took away the vacation benefits of four corrections officers who'd been in on the event.

*Tuvia Stern hosted a bar mitzah while in prison.*

# Comic Relief

*Looking for wisdom? Consider the words of these Borscht Belt comedians.*

"I once wanted to become an atheist, but I gave up—they have no holidays."
—**Henny Youngman**

"I could tell my parents hated me. My bath toys were a toaster and a radio."
—**Rodney Dangerfield**

"Anytime three New Yorkers get into a cab without an argument, a bank has just been robbed."
—**Phyllis Diller**

"My doctor is wonderful. Once, in 1955, when I couldn't afford an operation, he touched up the X-rays."
—**Joey Bishop**

"The guy who invented the first wheel was an idiot. The guy who invented the other three, he was a genius."
—**Sid Caesar**

"As the poet said, 'Only God can make a tree.' Probably because it's so hard to figure out how to get the bark on."
—**Woody Allen**

"An undertaker calls a son-in-law: 'About your mother-in-law, should we embalm her, cremate her, or bury her?' He says, 'Do all three. Don't take chances.'"
—**Myron Cohen**

"I don't exercise. If God had wanted me to bend over, he would have put diamonds on the floor."
—**Joan Rivers**

# The Apollo

*If you want the best entertainment in the best theater in the best city, check out the Apollo.*

*Burlesque artist Margie Hart performs at the Apollo.*

## It's Showtime

Harlem's Apollo Theater opened in 1914 as a burlesque hall, and even though it was located in the heart of New York City's most prominent African American neighborhood, blacks were not allowed to attend the shows. They didn't even perform at the theater until 1925, when, with the Harlem Renaissance in full bloom, whites began to recognize the value of black entertainment. But even as African American acts appeared on the playbill, the audience remained whites only.

The theater stayed that way until the early 1930s, when Mayor Fiorello La Guardia began a campaign to clean up New York City's vices and inadvertently created the most famous black theater in the United States. One of the "low-class" entertainments La Guardia wanted to get rid of was burlesque. (Another was organ grinders; he blamed them for causing traffic congestion and had them banned in 1936.) So in 1934, the Apollo's owner, Sidney Cohen, decided that instead of getting in the mayor's way, he'd change what kinds of shows played at his theater. In setting up the new playbill, Cohen also decided to cash in on the large, potential audience that lived in the neighborhoods surrounding the theater. That year, the Apollo "home of burlesque shows" became the Apollo "center of African American entertainment." For the first time in New York's history, blacks and whites attended the same shows and cheered for the same (black) entertainers: Billie Holiday, the Count Basie Orchestra, Bill "Bojangles" Robinson, and Bessie Smith, among others.

## Beware the Executioner

Since 1934, one of the most popular shows at the Apollo has been Amateur Night. Held every Wednesday, new singers, dancers, and comedians climb onto the theater's big stage to compete for prizes and, hopefully, to wow the audience. A good performance can make a career; a bad performance can kill it. And at the Apollo, it's the audience that decides good from bad. If the crowd doesn't like a performer on Amateur Night, they make it known—by yelling, jeering, heckling, stomping their feet, and, in the old days, occasionally throwing things. Then it's the job of a

*Aretha Franklin works the Apollo.*

man known as "the Executioner" to chase the unsuccessful contestants from the stage. Stagehand Norman Miller created the character in the 1930s. Today, the Executioner is played by singer and comedian C. P. Lacey.

Many Amateur Night performers have gone on to great careers. Seventeen-year-old Ella Fitzgerald made her singing debut on an Amateur Night in 1934. She'd originally planned to dance, but was so intimidated by a group that went before her that she chose to sing instead. The Executioner didn't come for Ella, and she went on to win first prize: $25. Other Amateur Night performers include Pearl Bailey, Dionne Warwick, James Brown, Sarah Vaughan, Jimi Hendrix, Gladys Knight, and the Jackson 5.

## Famous Fans

Tourists and Harlem residents aren't the only people who love the Apollo. The theater has some famous fans, too:

*Rod Stewart (left) and Nile Rodgers attend the Apollo Theater's 50th anniversary show.*

- In the 1930s and '40s, comedian Milton Berle used to take in shows at the Apollo, gauging crowd reaction, noting the comedians' timing, and applying what he'd learned to his own performances.

- In the 1970s, when Aretha Franklin performed at the Apollo, the marquee read "She's Home," because in the 1950s, long before she'd recorded any hit records, Franklin hung out at the theater. She came to watch and support her friends, like the Motown group the Four Tops.

- In 1964, on their first trip to the United States, the Beatles came to New York. When asked what they wanted to see in the city, the first thing they came up with was "a show at the Apollo."

## Equal Opportunity

Although the Apollo is known for nurturing black entertainers, many white performers have played on its stage, too. Among them: Buddy Holly, Rod Stewart, Boy George, and Joe Cocker.

*The famous Apollo Theater advertises its popular Amateur Night.*

# Gangs of New York

*"I would rather risk myself in an Indian fight than venture among these creatures after night."*—Frontier hero Davy Crockett, describing the gangs of Manhattan's Five Points

*Davy Crockett*

## The Gang's All Here

In the 1800s, one of the worst slums in the United States was in lower Manhattan, centered at the intersection of what are now Park, Worth, and Baxter streets. Called the Five Points (because the neighborhood used to be at the intersection of five streets), its tenements were damp, unhealthy, and built on landfill so their foundations were sinking into unstable ground. The people who lived there, mostly destitute Irish immigrants who'd come to America seeking a better life, couldn't afford to live anywhere else.

Typically, entire families in the Five Points were shoehorned into one small room, so many people spent a lot of time outside… and young men spent a lot of time in the streets. They had little education and few prospects for work, but the neighborhood had plenty of opportunities for drinking, gambling, brawling, and crime, making the Five Points one of America's first breeding grounds for powerful street gangs. Eventually, these gangs gained political clout and a public following, and when they went to war, it sometimes took the military to restore peace.

## The Forty Thieves

**Leader:** Edward Coleman

**Turf:** The neighborhood in and around Centre Street

**Claim to fame:** The Irish gang called the Forty Thieves was America's first known street gang, and it introduced organized crime to New York. The Forty Thieves met at a grocery store on Centre Street, but they never bought the rotting vegetables that the owner, Rosanna Peers, sold out front. Instead they gathered in the back room to drink rotgut liquor, and founding leader Edward Coleman used the store as his headquarters. From there, he kept track of the pickpockets, hold-up artists, and muggers that he'd sent out to terrorize the neighborhood.

Gang members were required to turn over their cash or stolen goods to Coleman. Anyone who didn't bring in money was thrown out of the gang immediately. And Coleman expected big earnings from anyone who worked for him—which led to his downfall.

In the 1830s, Coleman married a "hot corn girl," one of the young women who sold roasted ears of corn on the streets. In 1838, when she didn't bring in enough earnings, Coleman killed her. The murder shocked New York City, and Coleman—the city's first street-gang leader—also became the first person executed in the newly completed Tombs prison. The Forty Thieves continued for a while without Coleman, but its members gradually merged into newer, more powerful Irish gangs…like the Dead Rabbits.

*The first Tombs prison building, built in 1838, was the site of gangster Edward Coleman's execution.*

## The Dead Rabbits

**Leader:** John Morrissey

**Turf:** The entire Five Points

**Claim to fame:** The story of how the Dead Rabbits got their name is blurred with legends. One story says they began as part of the Roche (pronounced "roach") Guard Gang but, after a disagreement, split off into a group of their own. Supposedly that was when someone threw a rabbit corpse on the floor, and the new gang found its name. Another legend claims that the members carried a dead rabbit impaled on a pole when they battled other gangs. But in reality, it's probable that no bunnies were involved with the gang in any way.

"Rabbit" likely came from the Irish term *ráibéad,* which meant a "rowdy" or a "battler," and the term "dead" was 19th-century slang for "extremely." And the Dead Rabbits were definitely extremely rowdy fighters—they used brickbats, paving stones, clubs, knives, and guns to attack their rivals. They also used them to win elections.

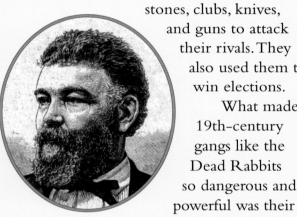

*John Morrissey*

What made 19th-century gangs like the Dead Rabbits so dangerous and powerful was their alliance with crooked politicians. Dead Rabbits were "shoulder-hitters"—thugs who helped to rig elections by intimidating voters and tampering with votes, destroying any ballot boxes and polling booths that favored an opposing candidate. As payment, the politicians forced police to look the other way when Dead Rabbits broke the law.

The Dead Rabbits backed pro-Irish, pro-Catholic candidates and Mayor Fernando Wood, elected in 1854, who claimed to be tough on crime but really was allied with the gang. That year, an anti-Irish, anti-Catholic gang called the Bowery Boys (see below) was trying to rig the election in support of its own Protestant candidate. At the time, the Dead Rabbits were led by John Morrissey, a tough, bare-knuckle boxer, who—along with his men—waylaid the Protestant supporters at the polls and saved Catholic ballots from being dumped in the East River. It worked. Wood was elected mayor, and to show his gratitude, he allowed Morrissey and the Dead Rabbits to open a gambling hall protected by his corrupt police force.

## The Bowery Boys

**Leader:** Bill "the Butcher" Poole
**Turf:** The Bowery, just north of the Five Points
**Claim to fame:** In the 1860s, the Bowery was a working-class neighborhood, and unlike lower Manhattan's other nearly destitute gangs, most of the Bowery Boys had steady jobs as butchers or mechanics. Bowery Boys had money to spend at their neighborhood's saloons, beer gardens, and dance halls. They could also dress well in hip stovepipe hats, frock coats, black flared pants, tall black boots, and even silk ascots.

*Above: Lower Manhattan and Five Points, c. 1850, was the turf of the Dead Rabbits.*

*Buggies navigate New York's Bowery in the late 19th century.*

Like their archenemies the Dead Rabbits, the Bowery Boys were shoulder-hitters. They might wear fancy clothes, but they'd steal and murder in the service of their political allies—in particular, the Know Nothing Party. This Protestant, anti-immigrant political party worked to repeal any laws that benefited the new Irish, German, and Jewish immigrants. The Know Nothings resented the immigrants—especially the Roman Catholic Irish, whose large numbers were seen as a threat to their jobs and way of life.

The most famous leader of the Bowery Boys, William "the Butcher" Poole, a native of Sussex County, New Jersey, was also a leader of the Know Nothings. Poole was, according to the *Brooklyn Eagle*, "a knock-down, gouging, biting, brutal savage." Once, in 1854, Poole confronted John Morrissey, his enemy from the Dead Rabbits, who was also a boxer. After exchanging insults, the leaders agreed to meet at a pier near Christopher Street for a bare-knuckle duel.

Morrissey arrived at the pier with a dozen of his friends…only to discover that the Butcher had hundreds of supporters with him. According to the *Daily Times* newspaper, Poole threw Morrissey to the ground and then beat, gouged, and bit him until Morrissey was forced to yell "Enough!" Morrissey and his pride were badly wounded. So in 1855, when Poole was shot to death, few people were surprised when Morrissey and his friends were accused of the murder. After three trials—all resulting in hung juries (rumors flew that political pals kept the Dead Rabbits out of jail)—the defendants went free. But the Bowery residents held a hero's funeral for Poole, whose last words were, "Good-bye, boys. I die a true American!"

## The End of an Era

In 1863 the Bowery Boys and the Dead Rabbits put aside their Catholic vs. Protestant feud and united—in their opposition to the Civil War. Many poor and working-class New Yorkers opposed Abraham Lincoln's Emancipation Proclamation because they feared freed slaves might come north and take their jobs. In addition, Congress had passed a conscription law, which allowed drafted men to pay $300 to stay out of the army, ensuring that the rich didn't have to fight. It was a sum well beyond most people in the Bowery and Five Points. In July 1863, the Dead Rabbits, the Bowery Boys, and several other smaller gangs joined in the draft riots. Buildings were looted and destroyed, and many of New York's African Americans were murdered. It took federal troops five days to quell the riot, which ultimately failed—the government refused to change the law, and both Bowery Boys and Dead Rabbits were drafted into the Union army. Although no one knows for sure if they all actually went to war, the gangs' numbers (and power) were diminished. By the time the war was over, newer gangs had already formed, and the Bowery Boys and Dead Rabbits gangs gradually disbanded.

# When Niagara Falls Shut Down

Park rangers get all sorts of silly questions, including "When do they turn off the water at Niagara Falls?" But in 1969, the answer was an astounding "In June." For five months that year, the U.S. Army Corps of Engineers diverted the water that typically flows over American Falls so that they could figure out how much the rocks underneath had eroded and could repair any damage.

*Workers halt the flow of Niagara Falls in 1969.*

# I See Space People

*A visit to Pine Bush, New York, a place that's become synonymous with things not of this Earth.*

*Dr. Bruce Cornet investigates UFOs.*

## We Made *The Enquirer*!

For at least 90 years, people in the tiny town of Pine Bush, 30 miles southwest of Poughkeepsie, have been witness to some strange phenomena: White orbs appear in the night sky amid a red mist. Mechanical rumblings emanate from deep underground. Strange lights illuminate farmers' fields. Gusty, warm winds blow out of the woods on freezing nights. And according to one observer, swirling lights hang suspended in the darkness "like a Ferris wheel on fire." In fact, there were so many eyewitness accounts in the 1980s—more than 2,000— that the *National Enquirer* proclaimed Pine Bush the world capital of UFO sightings.

*An amateur photo shows an alleged UFO sighting in Pine Bush.*

In 1992 a geologist named Bruce Cornet initiated an investigation…and concluded that several transmitters beneath Pine Bush send "photon beams" into space. Five years later, he recorded a strange boomerang-shaped object flying through the air accompanied by a stream of bright, white light. Cornet insisted it was an alien UFO.

## Bring in the Experts

But, the skeptics wondered, why not a more ordinary explanation…like an airplane? Pine Bush is only about 82 miles outside of New York City, one of the busiest air travel hubs in the world, and an airplane seemed logical. Cornet was ready to answer his critics:

- Lights from airplanes usually move in straight lines—the light from the boomerang swirled and jerked in a circular path.
- The boomerang was flying lower and slower than a conventional aircraft.
- In 2008 researchers from the History Channel examined Cornet's photos and interviewed him about the methods he used to capture them. Most important, they wanted to know if his camera could have been moving while he took the pictures, maybe *creating* those jerks and

swirls. But Cornet assured them that the camera had been secured on a tripod and that he'd controlled it with an electronic shutter release. After much investigation and study, they concluded that they couldn't determine what Cornet's photos actually showed.

## Space Tourists

These days, reports of strange lights and happenings in Pine Bush have declined, and some locals worry that they're losing their thunder to Wanaque, a town in northern New Jersey, where mysterious lights, flying disks, and other "interdimensional phenomena" have been reported since the 1960s. But Pine Bush still wears the title of New York's UFO capital proudly, and local businesses welcome terrestrial visitors hoping to find evidence of the extraterrestrial. The chamber of commerce hosts an annual "Pine Bush Area UFO Festival and Parade" and encourages "aliens and Earthlings alike [to dress in] UFO, alien, ET, space, and galactic-related costumes." T-shirts sporting images of big-headed, bulbous-eyed purple aliens are optional.

# New York's Finest...and Tallest

*They're part of the New York City scene and photographed almost as often as any local celebrity—here's introducing the horses (and the humans who ride them) in the NYPD Mounted Unit.*

*H. Ross Perot donated horses to the NYPD.*

## Bring 'Em Up from Down on the Farm

If you're ever near Central Park or Midtown, you might come across members of the NYPD Mounted Unit. These police officers and their four-legged equine partners patrol the streets, looking for criminals, providing crowd control for large events, and generally keeping order. The unit was founded in 1871 to deal with criminals in Central Park, and at one time, it boasted more than 700 officers on horseback. Their numbers began to dwindle at the dawn of the automobile age, though, and the unit was nearly disbanded in the 1970s due to budget cuts. But the NYPD loved its horses—and considered the Mounted Unit a valuable asset—so a group called the Police Foundation stepped in and saved the day, creating a program that allowed the unit to save money by accepting donated horses. Texas billionaire H. Ross Perot gave the department 12 animals; local nightclubs and restaurants—including the 21 Club, the Four Seasons, and Sardi's—followed his lead. Broadway star Bernadette Peters donated two animals, and a group of theater owners and banks chipped in to help with the rent on a Midtown stable.

These days, the department mostly buys its horses from places in Arkansas, upstate New York, and Pennsylvania. (At least one of the animals currently in the unit used to pull a buggy in Amish country.) Most of the mounts are castrated thoroughbreds and quarter horses that weigh between 1,200 and 1,500 pounds, and they're typically dark-hued horses of one color.

## New in the "Neigh-borhood"

The unit's ideal horse is intelligent, fearless, and friendly. Officials immediately pass over horses that bite, buck, or spook. Those that make the first cut are then tested at a stable in a quiet corner of the Bronx, where they're put through what's called "nuisance training." Walking shoulder

*Sergeant Tina Parrino of the NYPD Mounted Unit waters her horse at a Central Park fountain.*

to shoulder with older horses, the new recruits and their riders have to gallop across a blue plastic tarp and then march against a "crowd" waving trash bags and firing off air horns. The idea is to simulate the scary things that can happen in a city: a gun battle, a mass protest, or even the loud aftermath of a sporting event. Other tests include the use of smoke bombs, clanging metal pots, hissing flares, and the most important…blanks fired a few paces from a horse's head.

If a horse makes it through the early stages of testing and training (and only about one out of six does), then he is walked through the streets of quiet residential neighborhoods in the Bronx to get some low-key on-the-job training. Only after three to six months can the graduates leave the stable and make the 12-mile victory march to Manhattan, where they move into one of the unit's five stables and take up their assignments.

## Rider Attached

The police officers who ride the horses find it nearly as difficult to get a spot in the unit. There are many more applicants than openings because once in, most officers stay until they retire. The department has strict prerequisites for its hopeful applicants: Five years of experience on

*A mounted police officer patrols Central Park around 1900.*

the force, with at least two spent in high-crime neighborhoods. A cop who passes that particular hurdle then has to wait, sometimes years, for an opening.

When it comes, the officer is paired with a horse and the two begin training together. It sometimes takes two or three pairings for an officer to find the perfect equine partner (and vice versa), but once found, rider and horse often spend the rest of their careers together.

Today, the Mounted Unit employs about 60 horses and police officers. And although horses used to be given names such as "Zeus" or "Cherokee," these days it's more likely that a horse will be named for an officer killed in the line of duty. Several of the horses in today's Mounted Unit have the names of officers and firefighters who died in the 9/11 attack When Mounted Unit horses get too old to perform their duties, they retire to a farm in Orange County that the two-legged officers refer to as "horse heaven." Not bad for a lifetime of service.

# Woodstock Exposed

The Woodstock Music Festival—which ran from August 15 to 18, 1969, in Bethel, New York—remains one of the most iconic events of the 1960s hippie counterculture movement in America. But the event actually began as a capitalist venture, a way for four local music promoters to make enough money to open a music studio. John Roberts, Joel Rosenman, Artie Kornfield, and Michael Lang managed to line up some of the most successful musical acts of the time—Jimi Hendrix, the Who, Jefferson Airplane, Janis Joplin, and others—and entice hundreds of thousands of young music lovers to pay between $18 and $24 each ($108 to $144 today) to see them perform.

And don't think those artists played the show for free: They were paid anywhere from $10,000 (Credence Clearwater Revival) to $26,000 (Jimi Hendrix)…and several of them—like Janis Joplin, the Grateful Dead, and the Who—refused to take the stage until they'd gotten their checks.

*Janis Joplin parties at Woodstock.*

# Wow...What a Record!

*New York's people and places have been instrumental in setting some of the world's most amazing (and wacky) records.*

- **Record time for traveling the entire New York subway system:** 22 hours, 26 minutes, 2 seconds—set by British pharmacist Glen Bryant in 2014.

- **Most continuous upright spins on ice skates...on one foot:** 115, by Swiss skater Lucinda Ruh at the Sky Rink at Chelsea Piers, Manhattan, in 2003.

- **Oldest tennis ballboy at the U.S. Open:** Manny Hershkowitz (from Virginia), who was 82 when he worked at the 1999 tournament.

- **Smallest guitar:** 10 micrometers long (about 1/20 the width of a human hair), created by scientists at Cornell University in 1997.

- **Largest cup of hot chocolate:** 480 gallons, or about 8,000 cups (before marshmallows), created by the American Dairy Association & Dairy Council and displayed in Manhattan in 2010.

- **Most times jumping rope in an hour...underwater:** 900, by Ashrita Furman, from Queens, at the Gurney's Inn pool in Montauk, in 2001.

- **Smallest centipede:** the Hoffman's dwarf, which is 0.4 inch long and has 41 pairs of legs. Researchers from the American Natural History Museum collected 10 of them in Central Park in 1998.

- **Most expensive omelet:** the Zillion Dollar Lobster Frittata appeared on the menu at Norma's Restaurant at Le Parker Meridien Hotel in Manhattan in 2004. Ingredients: six eggs, a roasted Maine lobster tail, and 10 ounces of caviar. Price: $1,000.

*The world's most expensive omelet hails from Manhattan.*

## Blackout Stats

*On a hot July night in 1977, the entire city of New York went dark in a massive blackout.*

- Actual fires during the blackout: 1,037
- False alarms: 1,700
- Firefighters injured: between 45 and 55
- Cops on night duty on July 13: 2,500
- Cops on night duty on July 14: 12,000
- Sanitation Department staff mobilized on July 14: 3,800
- Number of 911 calls: 3,000 per hour (70,680 total)
- Amount given to NYC by the federal government to pay for damages: $11 million

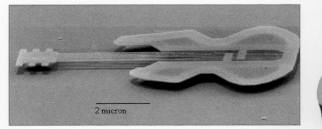

2 micron

*The world's smallest guitar originated in New York.*

*Lucinda Ruh*

# Smarter than the Average Berra

*Former New York Yankees catcher Lawrence Peter "Yogi" Berra is just as famous for his tendency to mangle the English language as for his epic home runs. Here are some Yogi-isms.*

- "A nickel ain't worth a dime anymore."
- "Always go to other people's funerals— otherwise they won't come to yours."
- "Baseball is ninety percent mental, and the other half is physical."
- "Even Napoleon had his Watergate."
- "He hits from both sides of the plate. He's amphibious."
- "I never said most of the things I said."
- "If the world was perfect, it wouldn't be."
- "I'm not going to buy my kids an encyclopedia. Let them walk to school like I did."
- "If people don't want to come out to the ballpark, nobody's gonna stop 'em."
- "In theory, there is no difference between theory and practice. In practice, there is."
- "The future ain't what it used to be."
- "You can observe a lot by just watching."
- "Nobody goes there anymore. It's too crowded."

## Berra Facts

- Yogi Berra played for 18 seasons with the New York Yankees (1946–63). He played on more pennant–winning (14) and World Series–winning (10) teams than any other player in Major League Baseball history.

- He got his nickname, "Yogi," from a childhood friend who, while watching a movie about an Indian snake charmer, said, "That yogi walks like…Berra!"

*Lawrence "Yogi" Berra strikes a pose.*

## Our Town

*Welcome to New York, home of Coney Island, the Catskills…and a lot of really strange town names.*

- Neversink
- Big Flats
- Busti
- Butternuts
- Result
- Coxsackie
- Hicksville
- Horseheads
- Root
- Mooers
- Pumpkin Hollow
- Tuxedo
- Gayhead
- Cat Elbow Corner
- Painted Post
- Hoosick
- Beaver Dams
- Podunk
- Place Corners
- Chili
- Yaphank
- Climax
- Owls Head
- Flushing
- Hogtown
- Pound Ridge
- Shinhopple
- Handsome Eddy
- North Pole
- Looneyville

# Got Diamonds?

*New York has everything: great theaters, great restaurants, great museums—and great diamonds…for cheap.*

A sculpture marks the entrance to the Diamond District.

- Of all the diamonds entering the United States, 90 percent of them come in through Manhattan's Diamond District, a one-block stretch of West 47th Street (between Fifth and Sixth Avenues) that's lined with buildings full of diamond merchants. It's one of the six major centers of the world's diamond industry. (The others are London, Antwerp, Johannesburg, Mubai, and Ramat Gan in Israel.)

- About 2,600 independent businesses operate in the Diamond District. But not all of them are actual stores—most are just booths in the 25 jewelry "exchanges" (institutions organized for the trading of diamonds and gems) scattered throughout the buildings on the block. Each exchange can house as many as 100 separate dealers, all with their own selections of merchandise.

- When dealers in the district sell to each other, they usually complete the transaction with a handshake and the traditional Yiddish phrase "*mazel und broche*," meaning "luck and blessing." Even in transactions that involve millions of dollars, there are rarely formal written contracts. In spite of the seemingly casual organization in the Diamond District, a single day's business can average $400 million.

- The diamond merchants sell to regular people, too, and according to many accounts, shopping in the Diamond District is like looking for a used car in a low-budget lot.

- According to one man who went there for an engagement ring, "The sellers—many of which have a thuggish quality to them—can be very upfront and aggressive…the salesmen are ubiquitous and will not simply let you browse. Some will even stand out on the street and openly solicit you for business if you so much as slow down near their door."

- So why shop there at all? Cost. In the Diamond District, buyers often pay half (or less) of what they would at a retail jewelry store.

- Buyers beware: A 2010 *New York Post* investigation found that booths in the jewelry exchanges can be rented short-term for as little as a day, making it difficult for buyers to distinguish shady dealers from reputable ones. Still, some of the biggest names in the diamond industry do business in the district, including the Gemological Institute of America and the Diamond Dealers Club.

- Merchants sell other kinds of jewelry

*The road to riches*

besides diamonds. Gold bracelets, gold earrings, pearls, rubies, and other precious metals and gems can all be bought there.

## Some Tips for Shopping in the Diamond District

- Sellers expect buyers to haggle. Don't accept the first price offered.

- Many won't take a check or credit cards. Bring cash. The "handshake" system is only for merchants. As a buyer, you should always get a receipt.

- Buy either a diamond that comes with a certificate of authenticity or one that the seller will allow to be certified on the spot. The exchanges all have appraisers who will certify a diamond for about $50. All deals should be contingent upon the diamond being appraised and certified.

- Usually, the most reputable diamond dealers have shops not at street level, but on higher, more secured floors. They can be hard to find. To locate them, you may need some sort of "in." (Basically, you have to "know a guy.")

- Watch out for trickery; disreputable merchants have been known to show a certificate for one stone while selling another. Others try to pass off synthetic stones as natural ones. According to one New York City blogger, buyers in the Diamond District need to remain alert and vigilant, do plenty of research before they go, and "know what they are doing!"

*Tourists and shoppers traverse Diamond Jewelry Way in New York's Diamond District.*

# NYU by the Numbers

- **3.63:** Average high school grade point average of the incoming 2011 undergraduate class.

- **10:** Percentage of NYU students who come from one of New York City's five boroughs.

- **32:** Ranking on the 2014 *U.S. News* "Best Colleges" list (out of 1,400 schools).

- **70:** Percentage of freshman applications that the school rejects each year.

- **$44,260:** Annual tuition for a freshman who enrolled at the business school in 2014. (That doesn't include about $15,000 for room and board, and $400 per semester for books.)

- **40,000+:** Undergraduate and graduate students.

- **$100,000:** Amount of private money it took to start the school in 1831.

- **$6.544 billion:** Amount it took to run the school in 2014.

# If Those Bleachers Could Talk

*From 1923 to 2008, the New York Yankees won 39 pennants and 26 World Series championships—more than any other professional sports team. And before the original Yankee Stadium was demolished in 2009, it was home to four of the greatest moments in baseball history.*

## April 18, 1923—Opening Day

The Yankees weren't always the winningest team in baseball. They began in 1901 as the Baltimore Orioles. After moving to New York two years later, they played at Hilltop Park as the Highlanders. They later changed their name to the Yankees and moved to the Polo Grounds in Manhattan, which they shared with (and rented from) another baseball team, the New York Giants. But for their first two decades, the Yankees couldn't catch fire. Most New Yorkers preferred the Giants, who'd

already won the World Series once. The Yankees hadn't even won a pennant, and they'd even been known to come in dead last.

Then, in 1920, the team's owners, Jake Ruppert and Tillinghast Huston, bought the contract of a talented slugger named Babe Ruth from the Boston Red Sox. Ruth's home runs brought the Yankees many wins and thousands of new fans.

Giants manager John McGraw (who didn't want to help out his successful competitors) evicted the Yankees from the Polo Grounds. So the Yankee owners bought 10 acres in the Bronx and built the biggest ballpark the country had ever seen…the first one to have three decks and the first to be called a "stadium."

Critics didn't think the Yankees had a chance of filling the stands—even

*Yankee Stadium attracts a crowd on opening day, 1923.*

84

*Babe Ruth swings during batting practice in 1935.*

with Ruth's help. McGraw predicted that the Yankees would starve because no baseball fan who could watch baseball in Manhattan would trek all the way to the Bronx—"Goatville." Yet when Yankee Stadium opened on April 18, 1923, "Goatville" was where the fans went. The grandstands were packed with 60,000 fans (most ballparks accommodated 30,000), who cheered as John Philip Sousa and the Seventh Regiment Band escorted the Yankees onto the field along with their archrivals, the Red Sox. And they watched Governor Alfred Smith throw the first pitch.

But most of the fans were really there to watch Babe Ruth. The stadium had already been nicknamed "the House that Ruth Built," because the team had taken such a gamble on his home runs filling the bleachers. Ruth had said, "I'd give a year of

my life to hit a home run in the first game in this new park." Sure enough, in the third inning, Ruth's bat connected with a pitch from Boston's Howard Ehmke. The ball went into the stands, and Ruth hit the first home run in the first game at Yankee Stadium. (Sure, the ballpark had been built so that its outfield fences favored left-handed hitters like Ruth—but still.) Sports followers took it as a sign that the Yankees were no longer the "other baseball team" in New York, and the Yankees went on to win the game, 4–1. Instead of starving, the Yankees won the pennant and their first World Series that year—defeating McGraw's Giants.

## September 30, 1927—Babe Ruth's 60th Home Run

Babe Ruth slugged 54 home runs in 1920, his first year as a Yankee, shattering the previous record of 29—which

he'd set himself while playing for the Red Sox. The next year, Ruth hit 59, breaking his record again. Then, for the next five years, Ruth pushed to take his home run record to 60.

In September 1927, that goal seemed out of reach. To get a record-breaking 60 home runs by the end of the season, Ruth needed to hit 17 in the season's final—a number that was more than most players managed in a season. But Ruth wasn't most players. By September 29, he had racked up an amazing 16 home runs.

On September 30, thousands watched as Ruth faced the Washington Senators at Yankee Stadium. It was the next-to-last game of the season, and Ruth was sitting on 59 homers—he needed only one more for a record-breaker. Seven innings passed, and no luck. Then, in the eighth inning, Ruth took a chance on a slow pitch from

*Babe Ruth (right) poses with Lou Gehrig.*

Tom Zachary and smashed a ball to far right field. The fans held their breath as the ball arced...and landed in the stands, just six inches inside the foul pole for a home run. As Ruth slowly circled the bases, fans danced, waved handkerchiefs, threw home-made confetti (torn from newspapers), and tossed their hats into the air.

After the game, Ruth felt content with his new record. He'd hit more home runs than any other *team* that season. Ruth predicted that it would be tough for anyone to beat him—and he was right: It was 34

years before another Yankee slugger, Roger Maris, broke the record with 61.

## July 4, 1939—Lou Gehrig Appreciation Day

As first baseman for the Yankees, Lou Gehrig was one of the best power hitters of his day, surpassed only by his teammate Babe Ruth. The native New Yorker set several batting records, but was most famous for playing in 2,130 consecutive games. After officially joining the team in June 1, 1925, he never

missed a game...for 14 years. Broken fingers and other injuries didn't stop him—he even showed up to bat on his wedding day.

But early in the 1939 season, Gehrig became so weak that on May 2 he simply couldn't play. Doctors at the Mayo Clinic in Minnesota told Gehrig that he had a degenerative neurological disease called ALS, or amyotrophic lateral sclerosis—now commonly known as Lou Gehrig's disease.

On July 4, 1939, between games of a doubleheader against the Washington Senators, the Yankees held a ceremony to honor the 34-year-old Gehrig. The crowd numbered 61,808—standing room only—and many people had come just to pay tribute to Gehrig. Yankees manager Joe McCarthy, New York mayor Fiorello La Guardia, Babe Ruth, and others delivered heartfelt speeches, and Gehrig himself gave one of the most famous and touching speeches in sports history. By the time he concluded, "So I close in saying that I might have had a bad break, but I have an awful lot to live for," many in the stadium were crying openly. Later that year, the Yankees also retired Gehrig's number (#4), the first time an MLB player had his number retired.

## July 2, 1941—Joe DiMaggio Sets the Record for Consecutive Games with a Hit

On May 15, 1941, with a single run against the Chicago White Sox, Joe DiMaggio began the greatest hitting streak in MLB history. Though he was already a Yankee superstar—who had led the team to four

*Joe DiMaggio swings for the fences.*

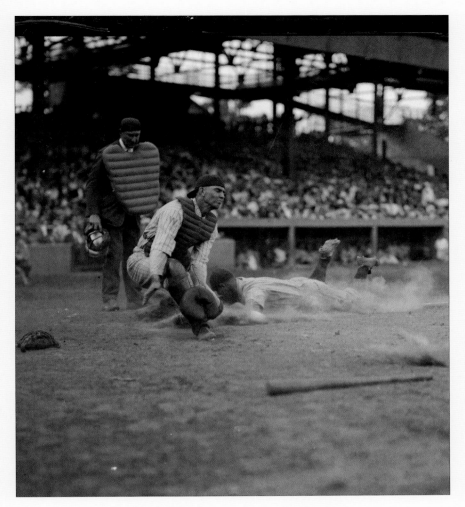

*Lou Gehrig slides into home base at Yankee Stadium.*

tied the MLB record that Willie Keeler had set in 1897. Many sports aficionados thought that Keeler's record couldn't be broken in the 20th century, due to tighter rules on foul balls being called as strikes, tiring night games, and long road trips that exhausted players. So on July 2, when the Yankee batters squared off against Boston Red Sox pitcher Dick Newsome, the huge crowd in Yankee Stadium, along with the entire country, wanted to see if "Joltin' Joe" could accomplish the impossible and surpass Keeler.

In his first chance, DiMaggio hit a line drive, but Boston outfielder Stan Spence made a spectacular catch, and DiMaggio was out. His next at bat came in the third inning, but he hit a ground ball fielded by third baseman Jim Tabor—another out. Finally, in the fifth inning, with a count of two balls and a strike, DiMaggio slugged a home run over the wall. The crowd jumped to its feet and erupted in cheers. Even the cynical press corps applauded. News went out over the radio that DiMaggio now held the major-league record for getting a hit in 45 consecutive games. In the end, Joe DiMaggio would hit safely in 56 consecutive games before his streak ended, a record that still stands today.

World Series titles between 1936 and 1940—it wasn't until DiMaggio got his 18th consecutive hit in a game against the Cleveland Indians a few weeks later that the *New York Times* began to keep track of the numbers. As his streak lengthened to 30 games, the public noticed, too. In a year when most news was about Adolf Hitler's invasion of Europe, DiMaggio's hitting streak dominated headlines. The first question addressed by newspapers, radio announcers, and even strangers on the street was often, "Did Joe get a hit today?"

When the streak went to 44 games, it

# Opening Lines

*Here are some more openings from some quintessentially New York books.*

*Edith Wharton as a child*

"On a January evening of the early seventies, Christine Nilsson was singing Faust at the Academy of Music in New York."

—**Edith Wharton,**
***The Age of Innocence***

"If you really want to hear about it, the first thing you'll probably want to know is where I was born, and what my lousy childhood was like, and how my parents were occupied and all before they had me, and all that David Copperfield kind of crap, but I don't feel like going into it, if you want to know the truth."

—**J. D. Salinger,**
***The Catcher in the Rye***

# New York's #1!

*It's no wonder that New York State is sometimes called "the center of the universe"—the state is the birthplace of many American firsts.*

*A model re-creates Robert Fulton's steamboat.*

## First Pizzeria

Grocery store owner Gennaro Lombardi received the first American merchant license for a pizzeria in 1905. Back then, pizza was called "tomato pie," and ingredients were piled upside down, with the cheese on the bottom, then anchovies (the only topping available), and the sauce last. A whole pie was 5¢, but Lombardi's would sell smaller pieces based on how much customers wanted to spend. The pie (or piece) was then wrapped in paper and tied with string.

## First Successful Steamboat

Steamboats were invented in America in 1787, but they weren't successful until 20 years later, when Robert Fulton built one that traveled up and down the Hudson River— 150 miles each way— without sinking.

Although it traveled at only five miles per hour, it ferried guests from New York City to Albany…in about 30 hours, with an overnight stop. Passengers feared the new technology, though—the boats spewed smoke, and people thought their boilers might explode—so the cost was only $3 (the same as older, much slower sailing ships), and included a cabin and meals.

## First Locomotive Railroad

In 1830 the Mohawk and Hudson Company started building a railway between Albany and Schenectady. It was America's first steam-powered railroad, though horses still pulled the train over certain parts of the track. Mohawk and Hudson conductor Billy Marshall made history when he got in a fistfight with the train's engineer and, upon winning, ensured that the conductor would manage a train's operations and crew, instead of the engineer.

## First Commercial 3-D Movie Showing

In June 1915, audiences donned cardboard red-and-green glasses and paid to see three one-reel films that tested the new medium of 3-D movies at the Astor Theatre on Broadway. They watched selected scenes from the crime drama *Jim the Penman*, shots of rural America, and scenes

*The boss in action (top) at Lombardi's, the oldest pizzeria in the country.*

NEW YORK

NEAR HERE
MOHAWK AND HUDSON
**FIRST RAILROAD**
CHARTERED IN THIS COUNTRY,
1826, BEGAN ITS RUN ALBANY
TO SCHENECTADY.

STATE EDUCATION
DEPARTMENT 1940

*This plaque now marks the spot of the first locomotive railroad.*

of Niagara Falls. The 3-D action was blurry, though, and reviewer Lynde Denig panned the experiment in *Moving Picture World*: "Images shimmered like reflections on a lake…it detracts from the plot."

## First Daily Yiddish Newspaper

Kasriel Sarasohn, a conservative rabbi in New York City, launched the *Tageblatt* ("Daily Page") in 1885 to serve the needs of the city's rapidly growing Jewish community. While most Yiddish newspapers were sold only in kosher stores, Sarasohn employed newsboys to peddle them on the streets alongside English-language papers, a move that got *Tageblatt* out to a wide audience and made it extremely popular.

## First Chess Tournament

Chess had been played in the New World since at least 1641, but it wasn't until 1843 that New York held the first chess tournament in America. Two years later, America got its first chess column, published by Englishman Charles Henry Stanley in New York's *Spirit of the Times* newspaper.

*New York chess columnist Charles Henry Stanley (left) plays a chess match with John Turner in 1850.*

## First State Park

During the industrial revolution, mills and factories were built along the Niagara River. To protect the area from pollution and further exploitation, the Niagara Reservation—a park containing American Falls, Bridal Veil Falls, and some of Horseshoe Falls—was formed in 1885. Instrumental in its creation was landscape architect Frederick Law Olmsted, who also designed Central Park. Now part of Niagara Falls State Park, the Niagara Reservation protects endangered peregrine falcons, lake sturgeon, bald eagles, and 14 rare plant species.

## First Car Registrations and License Plates

In 1901, New York mandated that all cars be registered with the state and display license plates. Vehicle registration numbers were issued by the state, but the plates were not—car owners made the plates themselves, out of everything from iron to leather.

## First Social Fraternity

Sometimes called the "Mother of Fraternities," Union College in Schenectady is where Kappa Alpha began in 1825 as the first general college fraternity. Other groups founded at Union College include Sigma Phi, Delta Phi, and Phi Beta Kappa.

*The Schenectady Pipe Band plays at a Union College graduation ceremony.*

# Talking about NYC

"New York attracts the most people in the world in the arts and professions. It also attracts them in other fields. Even the bums are talented."

**—Edmund Love**

"One day, there were four innocent people shot. That's the best shooting done in this town. Hard to find four innocent people in New York."

**—Will Rogers**

"This is New York, and there's no law against being annoying."

**—William Kunstler**

*William Kunstler*

89

# Birds of a Feather

*Helicopters and jets aren't the only frequent fliers in the city sky. New York is one of the world's best cities for bird-watching, and not just for pigeons.*

*A robin takes a bath in Central Park.*

## Bring Your Binoculars

Experts calculate that between 300 and 400 different species of birds migrate through or inhabit New York City each year. On an ordinary day, without trying too hard, a birder can see 75 to 100 species; in a year, if you work at it, you can see 200 to 300. Fairly easy to spot are herons, doves, orioles, wrens, woodpeckers, falcons, owls, mockingbirds, robins, and cardinals, to name just a few. And birders can track rarer species by checking out the New York Rare Bird Alert. For those who like to keep score, New York City Audubon organizes an annual Christmas Bird Count, in which teams count every bird seen in their assigned areas of the five boroughs—on a single day.

*A 1910 illustration identifies New York's plovers.*

## Why New York?

New York City is situated along the Atlantic Flyway, the coastal north–south migration route for millions of birds. During their long flights, the birds must rest and feed, and millions of them land in New York City's parks, gardens, and beaches. The city is also home to many year-round nesting and breeding species.

Habitat is the key: New York City has an astonishing number of habitats that are hospitable to birds. There are 1,700 public parks; freshwater marshes, lakes, and streams; saltwater beaches and marshes; rocky shorelines; estuaries; small islands; man-made ponds; private lawns; and even woodlands. Central Park is an outstanding bird-watching spot, an oasis for migrating and nesting birds, in which at least 285 species have been observed in recent years. The best spots for watching: around the water of the Harlem Meer, and in the woods and glades of the Ramble.

## Life on the Ledge

Across from Central Park, on the 12th-floor ledge of a luxury co-op building at 927 Fifth Avenue, is a large bird's nest made of twigs and sticks. Its builder and longtime tenant is a red-tailed hawk named Pale Male. He was first spotted in the park in 1991 and, as of 2014, had fathered at least 34 chicks with eight different mates. He was with his longtime mate, Lola, for eight years, and they raised seven chicks between 2002 and 2004.

Then disaster struck: In December 2004, the co-op board of 927 Fifth Avenue removed both the nest and the row of iron spikes that anchored it because some of the residents had complained about the bird droppings and meal "leftovers" from the hawks' diet of rodents and pigeons. Bird lovers—especially the New York City Audubon—were outraged, sparking protests and political speeches; actress Mary Tyler Moore (who lived in the building) even came out to support the hawks. The board finally relented, and Pale Male and Lola were allowed to rebuild their nest on the same spot. But even though Lola laid eggs every year after that, none of them hatched. Then, in 2010, Lola disappeared. Another female took her place but, sadly, died from eating a poisoned rat in 2012. Luckily, Pale Male got another chance for love with Octavia, his current mate.

Devoted New Yorkers continue to track the hawks with binoculars and through telescopes set up in Central Park, hoping to spy new chicks.

## Watch Your Step

Each spring and summer, a mile-long stretch of Rockaway Beach in Queens is declared off limits to everyone except a few Urban Park Rangers. The rangers' mission is to keep New Yorkers away from the breeding ground of the piping plovers, a species that's considered threatened in the Atlantic coastal area. In order to live and reproduce, these plump little grayish-white shorebirds need sandy beaches where they can find marine worms, beetles, mollusks, and other delicacies and where they can make nests and lay eggs safely.

What complicates their survival around humans is how effectively plovers use camouflage: Their nests (called scrapes) are small, barely noticeable depressions in the sand, often lined with bits of shell. Their eggs are speckled like sand, and their tiny hatched chicks are almost indistinguishable from the pebbles and twigs around the nests. One wrong step by a careless jogger could wipe out an entire plover home and family. Plovers were first discovered on Rockaway Beach in 1995, and with careful protection by the Urban Rangers, the rare bird's population in Rockaway continues to increase.

*New York City's famous hawk, Pale Male, and his chick nest on Fifth Avenue.*

# Rooms for Rebels

*The Chelsea Hotel has been a magnet for artists, writers, and other creative types for the last century, but it's in for some big changes.*

## What's in a Name?

Its *real* name is the Hotel Chelsea, but this New York landmark is better known as the Chelsea Hotel or just "the Chelsea." Twelve stories high, the redbrick building sits on 23rd Street, taking up a huge hunk of space between Seventh and Eighth Avenues in a neighborhood also called Chelsea. (The neighborhood came first and dates to about 1750, when a British officer bought the land and named it after…*something* in London. The "what" is disputed.)

The hotel began life spectacularly in 1884 as the Chelsea Home Club, one of New York's first cooperatively owned apartment buildings, or co-ops…at a time when there were fewer than 300 apartment buildings in New York. At the time, most middle-class people lived in single-family homes (row houses, brownstones, and so on)—apartment living for the middle class was a new idea. Members of the club could purchase one of the Chelsea's 70 units of three to nine rooms for $7,000 to $12,000. Each unit had high ceilings, wood-burning fireplaces, fire- and soundproof walls; some even had private penthouses. There were also 30 rental units that were designed to produce income for the co-op; they went for $50 to $100 per month. Most of the building's 100 units didn't have full kitchens, so the ground floor had a restaurant and several private dining rooms. The top floor had artists' studios and a roof garden. An impressive interior stairway swooped 12 stories up, lit by a large skylight.

In those days, the neighborhood around the Chelsea was a bustling theater district: Proctor's Theater (for vaudeville) was across the street; the Grand Opera House and others were nearby. But by the early 1890s, two major changes hit the Chelsea hard: Theaters began to relocate uptown, and a financial panic resulted in a depression. The Chelsea Home Club might have survived as a co-op if there hadn't been *another* financial panic in 1903. But in the uneasy economic climate, the place went bankrupt, and by 1905, the building had been bought and renamed the Hotel Chelsea.

*The Chelsea has been attracting tenants for more than 100 years.*

*Patti Smith (left) and actress Viva pose on a balcony of the Chelsea in 1971.*

## Artistic License

The Chelsea's reputation for attracting artsy tenants began soon after: Painters, writers, actors, and musicians discovered it, and they brought a certain bohemian cool with them. (Sarah Bernhardt and Lillie Langtry, two of the most famous actresses of the 1920s, often stayed there.) But history repeated itself and the hotel went bankrupt, so in 1939 a trio of partners—Hungarian immigrants Julius Krauss, Joseph Gross, and David Bard—bought the building. For the next 65 years, the Chelsea was a residential hotel: Tenants moved in (and were tossed out) at the discretion of the manager. Some stayed for short periods of time, some for decades, in accommodations that varied from a tiny room with a sink in the corner to a four-room suite with kitchen and private bath.

David Bard was the first manager, and his son Stanley took over the day-to-day operations in the mid-1950s. Stanley was an ever-present figure in the lobby, schmoozing with the residents, and became legendary for letting tenants slide with their rent when they were broke or short of cash. Stanley Bard was said to have a sixth sense about who was going to become famous (and therefore, whom to welcome to the hotel), and he didn't run a tight ship. The building wasn't kept up well or renovated. Tenants were pretty much left alone to live their lives. Stanley Bard's Chelsea was full of struggling artists who were just fine with the loose management style.

## The Glitterati and the Vicious

Probably the most notorious of the Chelsea Hotel's residents was Sex Pistols bassist Sid Vicious. On October 12, 1978, his girlfriend, Nancy Spungen, was stabbed in their room at the Chelsea, and Vicious was charged with the murder. He was later released on bail but died of a heroin overdose before the case could be tried.

Many other famous Chelsea residents also did famous things in the building:

- Welsh poet Dylan Thomas, 39, a long-time alcoholic and gravely ill with pneumonia, was staying at the Chelsea when he was rushed to the emergency room at nearby St. Vincent's and died there on November 9, 1953.

- Beat poet and author William Burroughs lived at the hotel in the 1950s and wrote some of his novel *Naked Lunch*, detailing the life of a heroin addict, at the Chelsea; it was published in 1959.

- After the 1960 breakup of his marriage to Marilyn Monroe, playwright Arthur Miller lived at the Chelsea for six years, during which time he wrote the play *After the Fall*.

- In 1966 Andy Warhol made a 3½-hour experimental "underground" film called *The Chelsea Girls*, using various rooms and locations in the hotel. The movie is supposedly about the Chelsea and its

*Renate Goebel's papier-mâché* Pink Lady *swings from the ceiling of the Chelsea Hotel's lobby.*

residents, but no one in the film except the poet Rene Ricard actually lived there at the time.

- Bob Dylan wrote his song "Sad-Eyed Lady of the Lowlands" at the hotel; it was released in 1966 as the final track on *Blonde on Blonde*.

- Musician Leonard Cohen met Janis Joplin in the elevator when he lived at the Chelsea. According to Cohen, they soon had a brief fling that he sang about on his track "Chelsea Hotel No. 2."

- In 1970 rocker Patti Smith and photographer Robert Mapplethorpe moved into room 1017 (reputed to be the smallest in the hotel). That's where Mapplethorpe took some of his earliest photographs—with a Polaroid camera loaned to him by another Chelsea resident.

*Leonard Cohen in 1974, the year he released "Chelsea Hotel No. 2"*

## Downhill Slide

By the 1980s, the Chelsea had become an unsavory place. According to rumors, it had an in-house heroin dealer who ran his business undisturbed; there was a brothel in one room; fires were a common occurrence, the result of passed-out occupants dropping lighted cigarettes; and more than one suicidal resident jumped into the 12-story well of the central staircase. But by the 1990s, gentrification was in full swing, and the rowdy crowds who had once flocked to the neighborhood were now drawn to cheaper apartments in other parts of the city and the outer boroughs. Unfortunately, this didn't do much for the future of the Chelsea. The hotel—despite being a beloved landmark—was shabby, run-down, and losing money. Things didn't get any better as the new century arrived.

On June 16, 2007, Stanley Bard turned 73 years old. It wasn't a happy birthday. He'd managed the Chelsea for more than 50 years and was expecting his own son to take over as manager after him. The Bards, after all, had been one of the Chelsea's original owner families. But out of the blue—or so says Stanley Bard—he was fired by the rest of the hotel's board members.

*A young Bob Dylan was inspired by his stay at the Chelsea Hotel.*

## Selling Out

To some, the ouster wasn't a complete surprise—the board had long been pressuring Bard to make the hotel more profitable. That hadn't happened, so they decided to get rid of him and bring in an outside management firm to run the Chelsea and to renovate, modernize, restore, and reinvigorate it. The new firm failed, and it was fired in less than a year. The next manager walked out after seven months, driven away in disgust by "incessant tenant harassment."

The board itself then assumed management of the hotel and stopped accepting long-term residents. Forty long-termers had already left after Stanley Bard was fired; about 90 were still in the hotel, and they claimed that the owners were trying to evict them by any means possible. The owners denied it, but rumor had it that the board was divided over how to run the hotel. Finally, on October 19, 2010, the board announced its intention to sell the Chelsea. Old tenants would be protected by New York City rent laws as long as their leases were in effect, but after that—no guarantees. The board's spokesperson said, "The history itself makes the hotel what it is…and there's nothing you want to do to change what the Chelsea is."

*Some of the Chelsea's visitors and staff pose in the hotel's lobby in 1968.*

# Seven Facts About the Statue of Liberty

*The Statue of Liberty has presided over New York Harbor since 1886. Most people know that she was a gift from France and that she's greeted millions of immigrants arriving in the United States. But here are a few facts that you might not know.*

*Frédéric Auguste Bartholdi*

## 1. She was born at a dinner party.

One night in the 1860s, French author Edouard de Laboulaye was entertaining some dinner-party guests when he came up with a grandiose idea: France and the United States should jointly build a monument honoring democracy and the friendship between the two countries. One of Laboulaye's guests, sculptor Frédéric Auguste Bartholdi, was so intrigued that he came up with the idea for the Statue of Liberty. Bartholdi officially named her *Liberty Enlightening the World* and hoped that the statue would enlighten his fellow Frenchmen about the importance of democracy in government.

## 2. She almost had no place to stand.

The Statue of Liberty is regarded as a treasure today, but when she was first built, many Americans had no use for her. The people of France raised about $400,000 so that Bartholdi could complete the monument, and the United States then had to raise about $100,000 for the pedestal. But by the time Lady Liberty was finished in 1884, the United States was having trouble coming up with the money. During the late 1800s, the nation was in the midst of a financial depression, and many Americans didn't want to pay good money for a statue that hadn't even been made at home. The *New York Times* complained, "No true patriot can countenance any such expenditures for bronze females in the present state of our finances." (The newspaper was mistaken about the metal—the Statue of Liberty is covered in copper.) Meanwhile, Congress refused to pay for the pedestal because the statue seemed more like a gift to the City of New York than to the entire country. And New York governor Grover Cleveland vetoed a $50,000 state grant for the pedestal.

Finally, in 1885, Joseph Pulitzer—owner of the *New York World* newspaper—wrote, "It would be an irrevocable disgrace to New York City and the American Republic to have France send us this splendid gift without our having provided even so much as a landing space for it." Claiming that the *World*'s working-class readers could save the day, he promised to publish in his paper the names of people who gave even small contributions to the pedestal fund. It worked. Donations poured in—more than 120,000 readers gave nearly $102,000 to place the statue on her pedestal.

*The Statue of Liberty is unveiled in 1886.*

### 3. She was a "First" Lady.

On October 28, 1886, the Statue of Liberty was installed on Bedloe's Island (now Liberty Island). There were fireworks and speeches from dignitaries, including President Grover Cleveland—who praised the statue that he'd failed to finance as governor. A month later, the Statue of Liberty became the country's first electric lighthouse when nine electric arc lamps were installed in her torch and five were placed around her star-shaped base. The torch, at 305 feet above sea level, was visible 24 miles out to sea. It acted as a navigational light until 1902.

### 4. She's thin-skinned.

Lady Liberty's outer copper coating is just 0.09 of an inch thick, thinner than two pennies. And her green color is the result of patina—tarnish on the copper.

### 5. Something's different about her foot.

Most humans have what experts call a "normal foot"—the "big" toe is the longest. But about 20 percent of people have what's called Morton's toe—meaning the second toe is longer than the big toe. (The condition is named for American orthopedist Dudley J. Morton, who discovered in the early 1900s that a short big toe could cause painful foot disorders.) But long before it was called Morton's toe, the condition was known as Grecian foot—because in classical and Renaissance art, a long second toe was considered to be beautiful. Bartholdi had always found inspiration in the statues of the ancient Greeks and Romans, so he designed Lady Liberty with one of the classic features of ancient Greek art: the Grecian foot.

### 6. She also wears a big shoe.

Bartholdi had always been drawn to large works, and he decided that his statue would be the largest since ancient times. (The largest in the ancient world was the 100-foot-tall Colossus of Rhodes, built during the third century B.C. and later destroyed in an earthquake.) The Statue of Liberty is just over 111 feet tall from her heel to the top of her head. Her face is 10 feet wide (Bartholdi used his mother as the model), her mouth is 3 feet wide, and her nose is 4½ feet long. Her bust measures 36 feet around, and her feet are 25 feet long, which, shoe experts say, makes her sandals the equivalent of size 879.

### 7. A poet changed her image.

Originally the Statue of Liberty was intended to be a simple symbol of democracy, but her proximity to Ellis Island also made her an icon of hope for new immigrants. Another reason for the symbolism is the

*Lady Liberty's "Grecian foot"*

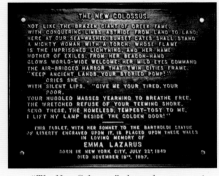
*"The New Colossus" plaque became part of the statue in 1903.*

poem "The New Colossus," which is inscribed on a plaque attached to the statue's pedestal. In the poem, Lady Liberty declares, "Give me your tired, your poor, your huddled masses yearning to breathe free."

But the poem didn't appear on the plaque until 1903. Its author, Emma Lazarus, worked with poverty-stricken Jewish immigrants who arrived in the United States after fleeing anti-Semitism in eastern Europe. She wrote "The New Colossus" for them in 1883. Four years later, Lazarus died and her poem was forgotten until it resurfaced in a Manhattan used bookstore several years later. People found it so moving that, more than 20 years after it was written, it became part of the statue.

# Bite Me

In 1996...
- 9,655 New Yorkers were bitten by dogs.
- 184 were bitten by rats.
- 1,102 were bitten by people.

# Loony Laws

*Most of the time, laws are important...they keep us safe and maintain order. But laws like these make us go "Huh?"*

- Statewide, it's illegal for women to go topless in public...but only if they're doing it for "business." (At all other times, it's okay).

- In New York City, you may not purposely throw a ball at someone's head.

- In New York City, honking a car horn in a non-emergency is illegal and subject to a $350 fine.

- An old law still on the books says that it's illegal for men in New York City to "look at a woman in that way" (i.e.,

*Donkeys are not allowed to do this in Brooklyn.*

flirt). If caught, guys can get a $25 fine for a first offense. For a second offense, they can be made to wear horse blinders every time they go out.

- In Brooklyn, donkeys are not permitted to sleep in bathtubs.

- It's illegal to carry an open can of spray paint in New York City.

- The New York Department of Health forbids people from growing poison ivy.

- If you want to take a bath in a pond in Sag Harbor, you must wear a bathing suit.

- Within the New York City limits, people may not keep mountain

lions, grizzly bears, or kinkajous as pets, and they may not dye their rabbits. (Cattle and pigs are okay, as long as they're fenced.)

- Statewide, the only people allowed to put you in handcuffs or leg irons are the police.

- People in Towanda may start fires in public parks, but only if they intend to cook something.

- More than three unrelated people may not live in one apartment in New York City.

- Milk sold in New York State may not contain pus, blood, manure, or vermin. (Maybe this one isn't so loony after all.)

*Kinkajous may be cute, but they can't be kept as pets in NYC.*

# The Botanical Garden Blossoms

*It's a place in the city where you can stop and smell the roses—but don't pick them! Here's how the Botanical Garden got its start.*

*The Perennial Garden in the Bronx*

In the late 1800s, Nathanial Lord Britton and Elizabeth Knight (husband-and-wife botany professors at Columbia University) went on a trip to England, where they visited London's Royal Botanic Garden. The pair was inspired to create a similar garden in New York City. With the help of the city and prominent financiers (like Andrew Carnegie and Cornelius Vanderbilt), they established the New York Botanical Garden in the Bronx on land that once belonged to a tobacco merchant named Pierre Lorillard. Today the 250-acre site is a U.S. National Historic Landmark and houses 50 gardens and collections containing more than one million plants, including...

- A 50-acre replica of the forest that once covered New York City.
- 30,000 trees, many more than 200 years old.
- An 11-acre azalea garden.
- 3,500 rose plants, in over 600 varieties.
- More than 8,000 orchids.
- 90 different kinds of lilacs in colors from white to pale blue to deep purple.
- A greenhouse that includes an ecotour of the world, highlighting tropical rain forests, deserts, carnivorous and aquatic plants, and one of the world's largest collections of palm trees.
- 100-year old tulip trees averaging 90 feet high.

*The Azalea Garden blooms.*

# Get Your (Everything) Here!

*Street vendors are as ubiquitous in New York City as World Series rings in the Yankees dugout. But where did all those food carts come from?*

## Opportunity Knocks

Food carts have been part of New York's street scene since the 17th century, but after the Civil War, when the city's population quintupled (from 400,000 to about two million by 1880), farmers living close by couldn't grow enough produce to feed everyone. Fruits and vegetables started coming into New York by rail and ship, and were delivered to wholesale markets, which also sold fish, olives, nuts, cheese, and other foodstuffs. At the end of the day, whatever the wholesale marketers couldn't sell to stores could be purchased for very little, so a new group of entrepreneurs emerged: peddlers who bought up the excess food and sold it from wooden pushcarts in the street. Pushcart vendors mostly sold surplus produce, but they also sold fresh and pickled fish, hot corn, hot sweet potatoes, hot chestnuts, pickles, pretzels, eggs, and even soda water.

## Life on the Street

Pushcart peddlers were legally forbidden from selling in one spot for more than 30 minutes, but to make it harder for the police to single out violators, the peddlers congregated in groups on streets like Hester, Orchard, and Grand on the Lower East Side. These open-air markets attracted crowds of local customers. Business was brisk, noisy, and nonstop, often lasting into the night. Most pushcart peddlers were immigrants—without speaking much English or raising much capital (renting a cart cost between 10¢ and 25¢ per day), they could work in familiar neighborhoods close to home. But it wasn't easy. Peddling was backbreaking

*An unemployed woman sells apples on a New York sidewalk during the Great Depression.*

*A mid-20th century vendor sells produce on Bleeker Street in New York.*

work for long hours in every kind of weather, and on a good day, a pushcart owner could make just enough to feed his family.

In 1900 there were about 25,000 pushcart peddlers all over the city. And by 1925 there were nearly 31,000 of them. Plus, 53 stationary open-air markets had sprung up around the city. During the Great Depression, with jobs so scarce, there were even more. In one of the most famous photographs of the Great Depression, a well-dressed former businessman sold apples for 5¢ each from a box on a city street corner. He was one of thousands.

## No Peddling Here

Local shopkeepers didn't like the pushcarts, though—they competed with stores, and aggressive peddlers sometimes drove customers away. The storeowners had support from very high places—including Mayor Fiorello La Guardia, who was known to hate pushcart peddlers, even the Good Humor ice cream men. In 1938 he confronted one at a public hearing, saying, "I'm going to abolish all itinerant peddling from the streets…I have to protect the city…This whole thing of pushcarts has been abused."

In 1936 La Guardia used federal money (which was pouring into the Depression-strapped city to create jobs) to build indoor markets that would get the pushcarts off the streets—a process that he called "professionalizing" the peddlers. The first opened on Park Avenue, between 111th and 116th Streets in East Harlem, and eventually, at least four others started up. But there was one major problem: The new market buildings didn't have enough room for all the peddlers. Plus, many of the vendors were unable to afford the $4-per-week fee charged for renting a stall. Thanks to La Guardia, the poorest peddlers were simply put out of work, and others weren't able to get a spot in the markets. By 1939 La Guardia had reduced the number of licensed peddlers from 6,000 to 2,700.

## Nice Try, No Cigar

The indoor market experiment was a huge failure. The stallholders hated all the rules and regulations: They had to wear neat white coats, keep their merchandise stacked in an orderly arrangement, and stay behind their counters while they did business. There was to be "no shouting or hawking by vendors nor abusive and lewd language." And, according to the new rules, they had to be American citizens.

Many of the vendors missed their previous lives on the street. And surprisingly, the shopkeepers missed them, too. As it turned out, the street peddlers had brought foot traffic to neighborhoods—shops all over New York City started to lose money for lack of customers. New Yorkers also missed the convenience, noise, low prices, and color of the street vendors. La Guardia's indoor markets didn't provide the same experience: They were scattered throughout the city (and there weren't many to begin with). So customers chose to shop at supermarkets and local groceries instead, and over the years, many peddlers chose to go back to selling on the sidewalks.

## License for Sale?

But the local government still didn't want all those vendors on city streets. They were hard to keep track of, and the city didn't have enough resources to make sure they all adhered to sanitation regulations. In

*Bakers work in the kitchen at La Marqueta, which first opened as the Park Avenue Market in 1936.*

1979, despite the fact that there was a huge demand for food-vending licenses, Mayor Ed Koch's administration capped the number at a very low 3,000. Before long, the waiting list for licenses was up to 10,000. As a result, from the 1980s on, many peddlers took to the streets illegally and without regulation. But vendors *wanted* licenses to avoid being fined or harassed by the police. And what's a street peddler to do if the city won't let him peddle legally?

He turns to a thriving black market in licenses. Today, there are only 3,100 legal licenses issued at one time, and a new one is issued only when someone gives up one of the 3,100. Licenses are good for two years and renewable as many times as the *original* license holder likes…for a fee of $200 per renewal. But a lot of the people who own those licenses don't actually vend. Instead, they make big money by illegally renting their licenses…for as much as $15,000 for two years. The black market is an open secret, and no city agency has cracked down on it. In 2006 the city council introduced legislation that would have raised the number of available licenses to 25,000. But at the end of 2009, after three years of discussion and debate, nothing had changed, and the number of licenses held at 3,100.

That doesn't mean the city just ignores unlicensed vendors, though. More than 60,000 vending-related tickets are written each year—sometimes for minor violations, like being more than 18 inches from the curb or neglecting to offer a receipt to a customer. The biggest ticket comes for failing to display a license in an easy-to-see place—that $1,000 fine can put a cart out of business.

## Food Fights

Vendors also get into turf wars with each other over who gets what space on what street, who's horning in on whose business, and how many vendors should occupy a given stretch of sidewalk. One vendor who sells baked goods from her truck had her tires slashed in 2007. She told the *New York Times*, "The street is like a playground when you're a kid, and you have to learn your way around." Another owner of a cupcake truck thought that cupcakes wouldn't be a problem for hot dog vendors. Wrong. He says, "When a hot dog guy sees a line in front of my truck, he thinks: 'That [should be] my line.'" Competition can even get violent: One vendor vying for a street corner in the Bronx followed his rival after work one night, pulled a knife on him, stole his money, slashed a tire on his food cart, and threatened to kill him.

*A Manhattan food cart offers pretzels, hot dogs, drinks, and snacks.*

## Rolling Stock

Most of today's street-food vendors sell their wares from four basic kinds of vehicles: processing carts and trucks and non-processing carts and trucks. Processing carts and trucks handle "the sale or distribution of any foods that require cooking or any other treatment, e.g., slicing, mixing, packaging, or any other alteration that exposes the food to possible contamination," says the Department of Health and Mental Hygiene (DOHMH), the city agency that regulates the carts and trucks. Examples: freshly made sandwiches or falafel, grilled meat or vegetables, roasted nuts, barbecue, or freshly squeezed fruit juice.

Nonprocessing carts and trucks handle only prepackaged foods or foods that don't need cooking. That includes whole fruits and vegetables, packaged snacks and ice cream, and—oddly enough—coffee and boiled hot dogs. (Hot dogs contain sodium nitrate, which acts as a preservative and protects against bacteria.)

*Mario Batali*

*Freddy Zeidaies*

Each kind of vehicle has to meet a slew of requirements about size, shape, structure, surfaces, equipment, and so on.

The DOHMH inspects every food cart and truck at least once a year and also spot-checks randomly, to be sure that food is being cooked and stored at the right temperatures, there's a clean water supply for hand-washing, the surfaces are sanitary, etc.

But the DOHMH inspection system isn't foolproof. Because street-food vending can have such a low profit margin, owners often cut corners to save a few dollars. For example, all licensed carts are *supposed* to go into a garage each night, where they're *supposed* to be thoroughly "showered." Vendors don't always do this—some leave their carts on the street all night.

## Best in Chow

Today, the street vendors even have their own Academy Awards... sort of. One day in 2003, some members of the Street Vendor Project—a legal-aid society for the city's vendors—were sitting around, discussing ways to raise money for the organization. They hit upon an idea: Why not hold a public awards ceremony for street vendors,

*The Nuchas food truck, owned by Ariel Barbouth, won Rookie Vendor of the Year in 2013.*

complete with judging and prizes for the best street food? The annual Vendy Awards were born, and the first competition and ceremony were held in 2005. Chef Mario Batali of *Iron Chef America* calls the Vendy Cup (the Vendy's grand prize) the "Oscar of food for the real New York."

The process works like this: Over a six-month period, customers send testimonials to the Street Vendor Project, nominating their favorite food vendors. The nominees are winnowed down to the 18 most popular, and those semifinalists gather in one place (Industry City in Brooklyn in 2013, Governor's Island in 2014) for a cook-off. The competition has five major awards: Best Street Food Vendor (the Vendy Cup), the People's Taste Award, Rookie Vendor of the Year, Best Market Vendor, and Best Dessert. Anyone can buy a ticket and attend the cook-off. In 2010 Fares "Freddy" Zeidaies, the King of Falafel & Shawarma, won both the first prize Vendy Cup *and* the People's Choice Award. Freddy, a West Bank Palestinian, started his cart in Astoria in 2002 and made it to the Vendy semifinals twice before winning. Like Freddy, many vendors today are immigrants— Dominican, Bangladeshi, Vietnamese— working long hours for minimal income, a lot like those early peddlers more than a century ago, who stood on street corners selling peaches and pickles and roasted potatoes to busy, hungry New Yorkers.

# Guerrillas in the Mist

Street art has come a long way since the 1980s, when gangs began tagging their territories in New York City's subways, storefronts, and just about anything they could put their spray cans to. But what was once a symbol of tough turf and unsavory characters has evolved into a legitimate art scene.

New York has become a favorite canvas for guerrilla artists because it provides a venue where their work can be seen by many people, especially those who might not typically venture into a gallery. It's also a way for them to make political statements or even brighten up city blocks that are otherwise considered "dumps."

These days, graffiti artists like Banksy, Shepard Fairey, and Nick Walker have become so popular that people from all around the world come to New York and other cities to see their work. In February 2011, fans of Nick Walker stood in line overnight to buy limited edition prints of his mural *The Morning After: New York*, painted on the side of a building at 35 Cooper Square in the East Village. The mural depicts a silhouetted man in a rowboat in New York Harbor looking at the city's skyline,

*A graffiti portrait of Tupac brightens up a New York street.*

which is dripping with graffiti paint. The building where the mural is painted is scheduled to be torn down...taking the mural with it and showing fans just how fleeting graffiti art can be.

# Disaster!

*A timeline of some of the biggest disasters in New York's history.*

## 1668:

A yellow fever epidemic hit New York City, one of the first recorded outbreaks of the mosquito-borne disease in colonial America. (The disease isn't endemic to the Americas; it was brought by the Europeans.) The number of fatalities is unknown, but Governor Francis Lovelace noted that "many people" died every day. Yellow fever epidemics occurred several more times in New York City; the last recorded outbreak came in 1870.

*Governor Francis Lovelace*

## 1836:

The *Mexico*, a ship that had departed from Liverpool, England, ran aground off Long Island on New Year's Eve. A rescue boat didn't arrive until the next afternoon, and 115 passengers and crew froze to death while waiting.

## 1896:

Temperatures in New York City rose above 90°F for 10 days—day *and* night. In the stifling heat, nearly 1,500 died, mostly as a result of crowded tenements and a citywide ban on sleeping outdoors.

## 1915:

A dynamite blast set off by subway workers under Seventh Avenue and 25th Street in Manhattan caused an entire block of the crowded street above to collapse. Seven people were killed; nearly 100 more were seriously injured.

*Rubble litters the street after the 1920 Wall Street bombing.*

## 1918:

A subway train derailed beneath Flatbush Avenue, Ocean Avenue, and Malbone Street. The "Malbone Street Wreck" killed 97 people, most of whom were heading home from work. It remains the worst subway wreck in history.

## 1920:

A bomb hidden in a horse-drawn carriage went off on Wall Street at noon. More than 300 were injured and 38 killed. The perpetrators were never found.

## 1928:

A defective switch caused a subway to derail underneath Times Square. The car smashed through a tunnel wall and was cut in half. The crash killed 16 and injured 100.

## 1957–65:

During this eight-year span, six passenger jets crashed in and around New York City, caused by a variety of electrical problems and pilot errors. The crashes killed 399 people, including passengers, crew, and six people on the ground.

## 1975:

On December 29, a bomb exploded in the crowded baggage claim area of LaGuardia Airport's TWA terminal. More than 70 holiday travelers were injured and 11 were killed. The bombing remains unsolved.

## 1990:

Avianca Flight 52 crashed at Cove Neck, Long Island, killing 73 of the 158 passengers and crew aboard.

## 1993:

A truck bomb exploded in the World Trade Center's underground garage, killing six and injuring more than a thousand.

## 1996:

TWA Flight 800 exploded 12 minutes after takeoff from JFK and crashed into the Atlantic Ocean south of Long Island. All 230 people onboard were killed. The explosion was at first thought to be a bomb, but was later determined to be an explosion of fuel vapors caused by an electrical short-circuit.

## 2001:

The 9/11 terrorist attacks by Al-Qaeda brought down the two 110-story World Trade Center towers and several surrounding buildings. A total of 2,996 people were killed, including the 19 attackers. It was the worst terrorist attack in U.S. history.

## 2001:

On November 21, American Airlines Flight 587 crashed into the Belle Harbor neighborhood of Queens shortly after takeoff from JFK Airport, killing all 260 on board and five people on the ground. The cause was later determined to be the result of turbulence from another plane and overuse of the rudder by the pilot.

## 2003:

The Staten Island Ferry crashed into a pier at the St. George Ferry Terminal of Staten Island, killing 11 and injuring 70.

## 2009:

On January 15, U.S. Airways Flight 1549 flew into a flock of Canada geese, causing both engines to fail. Captain Chesley "Sully" Sullenberger carefully ditched the plane

*Flight 1549 landed safely in the Hudson River in 2009.*

in the Hudson River—and all of the 155 people on board survived. One member of the National Transportation Safety Board said, "It has to go down [as] the most successful ditching in aviation history."

*Investigators reconstruct the wreckage of TWA Flight 800 to determine the cause of the crash.*

*Terrorists attack the World Trade Center in 2001.*

# On the Run

*Think it's hard to get a hotel room in New York at Christmastime? Just try getting one during the marathon.*

*Fred Lebow jogs in Central Park.*

## Marathon Man

The New York City Marathon, run every November, is the largest in the world—in 2010, 45,344 runners participated in the race, cheered on by 2.5 million spectators lining the streets. Its 26.2-mile course takes the runners through all five boroughs: The race starts on the Staten Island side of the Verrazano–Narrows Bridge and then snakes through Brooklyn, crosses the Pulaski Bridge into Queens, goes over the Queensboro Bridge into Manhattan, swings briefly through the Bronx, and then returns to Manhattan for the last five or so miles, ending in Central Park.

New York City owes its world-renowned feat of footwork to one man: Fred Lebow (born Fischel Lebowitz in Romania in 1932), who took up running in the late 1960s, hoping it would improve his tennis game. Running soon replaced tennis as his passion, though, and he agreed to become the (unpaid) president of the New York Road Runners, a running club that sponsors many races and events. Lebow organized the first New York City Marathon in 1970: a four-loop race in Central Park with only 127 starters, 55 finishers (Lebow finished 45th), and very few spectators. The entrance fee was $1, and the prizes were wristwatches that Lebow bought himself. But it was a beginning, and over time, the marathon became an annual—if modest—event.

## Off and Running

In 1976 Lebow convinced the city to allow a five-borough race, and he knew it had to be a major success if it was going to get enough support to continue. Lebow lined up a few sponsors (such as *New Times* magazine), a pair of American marathon stars (Bill Rodgers and Frank Shorter), and 2,000 runners. Crowds came out to cheer, the media covered the event, and Fred Lebow and the New York City Marathon were off and running. Each year, the race got more popular and received more press coverage.

In 1992 Fred Lebow, who had been battling brain cancer, ran his last race. He ran slowly—his finish time was 5 hours, 32 minutes, and 34 seconds—and was accompanied by nine-time marathon winner Grete Waitz. Lebow died two years later, on October 9, 1994. At his memorial service, Mayor Rudy Giuliani and the president of the New York Road Runners, which still sponsors the marathon, led 3,000 mourners in a march across the race's Central Park finish line.

## Winning the Lottery

There are three main types of participants in the marathon, though everyone must be over 18: elite runners (proven world-class winners with top-level times from a variety of races); AWDs (athletes with disabilities like impaired vision or prosthetic limbs, or conditions requiring wheelchairs or handcycles); and everyone else. Each runner wears an identifying number and attaches a computer chip to one shoe to record when he or she crosses the start and finish lines.

*The New York City Marathon accepts just 45,000 of the 60,000 runners who apply.*

The famous runners—like Olympic champion Haile Gebrselassie of Ethiopia—are invited to participate; so are some special people, like rescued Chilean miner Edison Peña in 2010. But for most people, getting into the race is tough. They're selected by lottery—more than 60,000 runners apply for spots, and about 45,000 get chosen.

But if you're not an invited runner and you don't want to depend on winning the lottery to secure a spot, there are some other ways you can be guaranteed an entry to the marathon:

• If you run a qualifying marathon a year before and your time is good enough to meet the official standards (published by January 1), even if you're not a world-class competitor.

• If you agree to raise money for one of the marathon's official charities.

• If you've gotten an entry before and had to cancel before the race.

• If you're a member of New York Road Runners, have completed at least nine qualifying races, and have volunteered at one event during the previous year.

• If you've completed 15 or more New York City Marathons.

• If you've been denied an entry for the last three years in a row.

What's included if you do get a spot, aside from the thrill of running with the pack? You get transportation to the starting line; a ticket to the "start festival" (breakfast, entertainment, and religious services); medical support; hydration; a goody bag; an official handbook; a medal, food,

beverages, and a silver "heat sheet" at the finish to help you cool down; and an official finisher certificate.

## Marathon Stats

• Along the course, 24 official fluid stations dispense 62,370 gallons of water and 32,040 gallons of Gatorade in 2.3 million recyclable cups. (Eleven tons of trash are collected from the fluid stations after the race.) Portable toilets can be found every mile, starting at mile 3. And "sweep" buses follow the runners to transport any dropouts to the finishing area in Manhattan.

• There hadn't been a marathon-related death since 1994, but in 2008, there were three: One runner had a heart attack at mile 22 and died 11 days later; a runner with a preexisting heart condition had a fatal heart attack right after completing the race; and a third died of a heart attack several hours after the race.

• Slowest race time: In 2000 Zoe Koplowitz, who had multiple sclerosis and diabetes, finished in 35 hours, 27 minutes.

• Men's fastest time: 2:05:06, in 2011, by Geoffrey Mutai of Kenya. Women's fastest time: 2:22:31, by Margaret Okayo of Kenya in 2003.

• Men's prize money: 2014 men's winner was Geoffrey Mutai (again!), who finished in 2:08:24 and took home $100,000. The 2014 women's winner Priscah Jeptoo, also of Kenya, finished in 2:25:07 and received $100,000.

# Home Sweet Home

In the 1998 movie *Godzilla*, the enormous, menacing lizard made a nest for its 200 eggs inside Madison Square Garden.

# There Goes the Neighborhood: Queens

*If you've ever wondered why that neighborhood is called that, here's why.*

A drawing shows King Charles II of England and Queen Catherine, for whom Queens is named.

- The Dutch settled **Queens** in the early 1600s, but it didn't get its modern name until after the British moved in. It was originally part of an area called Yorkshire, but in 1683, the borough (and its county) were renamed Queens for Queen Catherine, the wife of England's King Charles II.

- **Blissville** was named for Neziah Bliss, a shipbuilder and entrepreneur. In the 1830s and '40s, Bliss owned the land where the neighborhood now sits.

- **Flushing** began in 1645 as a Dutch settlement. The area was originally named Vlissingen after a port in the Netherlands, but the British thought the word sounded like "flushing," so when they took over, they renamed the town. In 1657 Quakers living in Flushing rebelled against Governor Peter Stuyvesant's decree that Dutch Reformism was the only religion colonists could practice. The Quakers drafted the "Flushing Remonstrance," arguing for religious freedom. Stuyvesant retaliated against the Quakers, arresting and fining those who refused to give up their religion. But some historians believe that the document was an inspiration for the creation of the First Amendment to the U.S. Constitution, written more than 100 years later.

- A "neck" is an elongated piece of land, so **Little Neck** is part of a small piece of land—which also includes Douglaston—that protrudes into Little Neck Bay of Long Island Sound.

- **Jamaica** comes from the English name for the Native American tribe that lived there: the Jameco. (Jamaica Avenue is an old Indian road and was, at one time, the only way to get from Queens to Brooklyn.)

Built in 1694, the Old Quaker Meeting House in Flushing is New York City's oldest church.

Peter Stuyvesant

*The lobby of the former Loew's Valencia Theater (above) in Jamaica, Queens, has not changed much over the years, but the building is now a church (left).*

# N.Y. Bumper Stickers

- Smile if you love Wall Street.
- I'm from New York, and you talk too slow.
- This vehicle is protected by an anti-theft sticker.
- Keep New York beautiful. Dump your trash in Jersey.
- Support bacteria: It's the only culture some people have.

# Radio City

*Every great city needs a great public radio station, and WNYC is New York City's. Here's a timeline of the station's history.*

A painting of Grover Whalen made the cover of Time *magazine, 1939.*

Mayor La Guardia hosts his Talk to the People *program on WNYC.*

### 1922–24:

Regularly scheduled commercial radio broadcasting started in America around 1920. But New York City had no public-owned station even in the works until 1922, when Grover A. Whalen—Commissioner for Plants and Structures—convinced the city to approve $50,000 for a "Municipal Wireless Broadcasting Station." It took two more years for Whalen to wrangle a transmitter: He finally located one in Brazil and had it shipped to New York. Nonprofit, noncommercial, municipally funded WNYC-AM hit the airwaves on July 8, 1924, and New York became one of the first city governments in the country to be directly involved in radio broadcasting.

### 1926–29:

WNYC, run by Commissioner Whalen, made radio history in 1926 when it aired radio's first quiz program, *The Current Events Bee*, and covered Admiral Richard E. Byrd's return from his legendary flight to the North Pole. In 1927 the station

*The Manhattan Municipal Building on Centre Street was WNYC's home from 1922 to 2008.*

reported Charles Lindbergh's landing in New York after his solo flight to Paris, and two years later, it introduced *The Masterwork Hour*, the longest-lasting program of recorded classical music on radio.

### 1938–43:

In 1938 Mayor La Guardia created a special city agency (the Municipal Broadcasting System) to run the station, and on

*The USS* Arizona *sinks after the Japanese bombed Pearl Harbor in 1941. WYNC was the first American outlet to report the attack.*

December 7, 1941, WNYC was the first U.S. station to report the bombing of Pearl Harbor by the Japanese. WNYC was still just a tinny-sounding daytime-only AM station, though; it wasn't until it added FM in 1943 that it was able to broadcast higher-quality sound around the clock. WNYC-FM was the only FM station in the country to create programs specifically for FM, like *Nights at the Ballet* from the orchestras of the Metropolitan Opera and New York City Center, and live opera broadcasts from City Center Opera Company.

## 1945:

In one of the station's most iconic moments, during a newspaper strike, Mayor La Guardia started reading the newspaper cartoons *Dick Tracy* and *Little Orphan Annie* to the city's children. He read only three times, but the concept became a regularly featured program called *The Comic Parade*, with comedians doing the readings.

## 1970–79:

Hard times came with the city's fiscal problems of the 1970s. Mayor John Lindsay cut WNYC's funding, and 55 staffers had to be laid off. The relationship between the city and its broadcast media was an uneasy one: The stations (WNYC-AM and FM, and WNYC-TV) depended on the city for money, and that made them vulnerable both to cutbacks and to political pressure. The stations' head, Mary Perot Nichols, was worried, and in 1979 she started raising money from private sources so that the stations could survive the city's cutbacks.

It was also becoming difficult to shield the stations from political pressure. In the same year that Nichols established the foundation, Mayor Ed Koch introduced the "John Hour"—he wanted WNYC to broadcast the names of men ("johns") who were arrested for soliciting prostitutes. Station management was furious, announcers threatened to walk out, and the idea was ditched after just one broadcast. But this was not the last time a mayor tried to influence the radio station.

## 1994–96:

Newly elected mayor Rudy Giuliani thought the city shouldn't be in the broadcasting business at all, and his transition team recommended selling the valuable WNYC radio and TV licenses to a private company. Giuliani offered two options to the station: sell all or part of the WNYC "assets" (AM, FM, and the TV station), or find a way to make the entire group self-sufficient. In the end, the mayor compromised: The city turned over the licenses for WNYC-AM and WNYC-FM to a non-profit group called the WNYC Foundation—for a price of $20 million. The foundation had six years to raise the money and could stay rent-free in its studios in the Municipal Building on Centre Street. WNYC-TV was sold to a partnership of Dow Jones & Company and ITT Corporation for $207 million.

*A WNYC reporter goes after a story.*

*Mayor Ed Koch joins WNYC in celebrating 60 years on the the air in 1984.*

## 2001–02:

The last payment from the WNYC Foundation to the city for the radio stations was due in January 2002, but just as management was planning the final fund drives, September 11, 2001, stopped everything in its tracks.

On 9/11, WNYC's FM and backup transmitters went down with the twin towers. The staffers had to evacuate their offices (which were close to ground zero) and couldn't return for three weeks. They camped out at NPR's offices in Midtown, and continued broadcasting via an AM signal and by a live Internet stream. In the wake of the attacks, the station was averaging more than a million listeners per week—the first time any public radio station had seen such high numbers. But as a result of the attacks, WNYC had to raise more than

$4 million to replace the destroyed transmitters and get itself back on the air full-time—at the same time that it was trying to raise the last payment to the city. An emergency on-air fund-raiser in October pulled in the money for the new transmitters, but the January 2002 fund drive for the final payment to the city came up short. It took until the spring of 2002 to finish paying off the city and achieve complete autonomy.

But with independence came trouble: staff shake-ups and resignations, abrupt changes in programming, and constant pressure to raise enough money to keep the stations going. Many loyal listeners were confused—even outraged by the changes, especially when the station eliminated five hours of daytime classical music in favor of news and cultural shows.

## 2006–08:

But even bigger plans were in the works: In 2006 CEO Laura Walker announced that the station would leave its dilapidated old home in the Municipal Building and move to a brand-new space across town at 160 Varick Street.

The old Municipal Building studios were inconvenient and scattered over eight floors, the front-door security lines were frustrating for guests coming for interviews, and there were endless maintenance problems. The Varick Street space would give the station 2½ floors of new offices, twice as many recording studios and recording booths, and a lot more square footage. And there would be a 140-seat street-level studio for live broadcasts and other special events. It was expensive (about $61.3 million for rent, renovation, and new programming), but the 189 staffers were eager for the improvements. At 10 a.m. on June 17, 2008, roughly two years after the move was announced, Brian Lehrer, host of the popular Brian Lehrer Show for more than 20 years, flipped the "On Air" switch in the new building and the move was complete.

## 2009–14:

In October 2009, WNYC acquired WQXR, a well-known classical music station. With WQXR in the fold, WNYC-FM dropped the remainder of its classical music programming and switched to round-the-clock news and information.

Today, New York's public radio station has podcasting, live streaming, and a handful of prestigious Peabody Awards for broadcasting excellence. It's one of National Public Radio's most important customers—WNYC has more than 100,000 paying members, with many nonprofit foundations and other entities adding to its funding. It reaches more than 1.6 million listeners each week—the largest public radio audience in the country— and it's the most-listened-to station in Manhattan. Its stated mission is "to make the mind more curious, the heart more tolerant, and the spirit more joyful through excellent radio programming."

# Deep Thoughts from Jerry Seinfeld

"Make no mistake about why these babies are here—they are here to replace us."

"Now they show you how detergents take out bloodstains, a pretty violent image there. I think if you've got a T-shirt with a bloodstain all over it, maybe laundry isn't your biggest problem."

"Where lipstick is concerned, the important thing is not color, but to accept God's final word on where your lips end."

"It's amazing that the amount of news that happens in the world every day always just exactly fits the newspaper."

"The big advantage of a book is it's very easy to rewind. Close it and you're right back at the beginning."

"I was the best man at the wedding. If I'm the best man, why is she marrying him?"

"Dogs are the leaders of the planet. If you see two life-forms, one of them's making a poop, the other one's carrying it for him, who would you assume is in charge?"

# The Naked Cowboy

*When it comes to tourist attractions, New York City has some of the most spectacular: the Empire State Building, the Statue of Liberty, the Brooklyn Bridge...and this guy.*

*The Naked Cowboy performs in Times Square.*

## Dude in the Nude

Street performers in New York City are a dime a dozen. No matter the corner, the time of day, or the weather, buskers are always out—singing, doing flips and other gymnastics, break-dancing, even miming to earn a buck. But since the early 2000s, visitors to Times Square have been entertained by a unique performer whom the New York State Tourism Department has called "more recognizable than the Statue of Liberty." Who is he? The Naked Cowboy, of course.

It all began in Southern California in 1997, when a recent college graduate named Robert John Burck dressed up like a cowboy, took his guitar to the boardwalk in Venice Beach, and started playing for tips. He made only a dollar, but a friend suggested that he try again—wearing just his underwear—and see if that made a difference. It did. Says Burck, "I made $100 and a TV crew came out and filmed me."

## "King of Planet Earth"

Pretty soon, Burck had taken his show on the road. He landed in New York City and set up a "performance space" in the middle of Times Square. His schtick was simple: Rain or shine, sleet or snow, he wore only a cowboy hat, cowboy boots, and tighty-whiteys with the words "Naked Cowboy" stenciled on the back in red, white, and blue. He also carried a guitar, which he placed "strategically" in photos to make it look like he was wearing nothing at all. He posed for pictures, played music (including his original songs "Naked Cowboy" and "Balls of Steel"), and became a popular stop on New York City bus tours. Visitors lined up to see him, hot dog vendors loved the business he brought in, and NYPD cops came by to say hello.

By 2005 Burck was making up to $1,000 a day, and he had the ego to match. When one reporter asked what kind of performer he considered himself to be (singer, actor, busker, etc.), Burck replied simply, "I'm the king of planet Earth."

## More than just a Pretty Face

Burck was a savvy businessman who trademarked his stage name and its female variant (the Naked Cowboy *and* Naked Cowgirl) and had a keen eye for branding. While building his business, he sent out thousands of postcards each month to friends and acquaintances to remind them of who he was and what he did. (The picture showed him in the middle of Times Square, surrounded by his adoring public.)

He also had his eye on bigger and better things. In 2009 Burck announced that he planned to challenge Michael Bloomberg in the mayoral race. He had to drop out because he hadn't filled out the proper paperwork, but politics remained in his sights. The next year, a freshly shaven Burck (fully dressed in a suit and tie) announced that he would be a 2012 Republican primary presidential candidate, running for the Tea Party. Why? According to Burck, "Politicians are selling out America and its most cherished institution, that being capitalism." Reporters didn't take Burck's announcement seriously, peppering him with questions like "Where's your underwear?" and "Aren't you just another dishonest politician since you're not *technically* naked while performing in Times Square?" But Burck waved them off, announcing that he had "no time for games." Soon after, he was back on the street in his tighty-whiteys, guitar in hand.

# Madison Square Garden Did It First

*"The World's Most Famous Arena" has hosted countless star-studded events since opening its doors in 1874. Come along as we celebrate some of the fabulous firsts that have happened at the Garden over the past 130+ years.*

*George Harrison plays at the Concert for Bangladesh in 1971.*

## North America's First Artificial Ice Rink

Madison Square Garden was transformed into a winter wonderland on February 12, 1879, with the installation of a 6,000-square-foot indoor ice rink, the first in North America. The opening coincided with a gala ice carnival that attracted thousands of revelers to the arena.

## First Indoor Football Game

Football came in out of the cold on December 28, 1902, when Syracuse defeated "New York" (a team made up of several professional football players from around the state) in the inaugural game of the World Series of Pro Football. Organized by the Garden's operations manager, Tom O'Rourke, the innovative event was an attempt to attract patrons to the building during its slowest time of the year. Unfortunately, New Yorkers continued to stay away in droves, and the short-lived, six-day series was discontinued in 1904.

*The Jackson 5 appear on the* Ed Sullivan Show *three months after their television debut at Madison Square Garden.*

## First Televised Basketball Game

Basketball made its small-screen debut on February 28, 1940, when the local NBC affiliate W2XBS broadcast a regular-season game between Fordham University and the University of Pittsburgh live from Madison Square Garden. Only one camera was used in the no-frills telecast as the Fordham Rams defeated Pitt's Panthers, 57–37.

## The Jackson 5's First Television Appearance

The pop group was still relatively unknown on August 22, 1969, when they made their

television debut at the Miss Black America Pageant at Madison Square Garden. The event gave the group some much-needed exposure and paved the way for a series of sold-out Michael Jackson shows at the Garden over the next four decades.

## First Special Benefit Concert

The Garden made headlines around the world on August 1, 1971, when it played host to the Concert for Bangladesh, the first humanitarian benefit concert. Organized by former Beatle George Harrison and featuring artists like Eric Clapton, Bob Dylan, Billy

*WrestleMania champion Hulk Hogan in 2014*

Preston, and Ringo Starr, the one-day event raised money for Bangladeshi refugees victimized by the 1970 Bhola cyclone and the bloody fallout from the Bangladesh Liberation War. The initiative generated more than $243,000 in ticket sales and led to the creation of future benefit concerts such as Live Aid and Farm Aid.

## First WrestleMania

Big-time wrestling overtook the Garden on March 31, 1985, when the World Wrestling Federation presented its first WrestleMania. Billed as "The greatest wrestling event of all time," the show featured nine wrestling matches, including a heavily hyped tag-team bout with Hulk Hogan and Mr. T battling another team. (Hogan's side won.) WrestleMania has since become an annual tradition that attracts millions of viewers each year.

## First HDTV Scoreboard

In October 2000 the Garden changed the way fans watch live sporting events when it installed the world's first high-definition scoreboard system. Unveiled at the New York Rangers' regular-season opener, the system included four huge screens on the Garden's main hanging structure and 150 smaller screens scattered throughout the building. Other arenas around the world have since followed the Garden's lead in an attempt to give fans crisper images and higher-resolution replays.

*Below: Derek Stepan of the New York Rangers guards the puck from Drew Doughty of the Los Angeles Kings at Madison Square Garden during a 2014 game.*

# On Broadway

"Being on Broadway is the modern equivalent of being a monk. I sleep a lot, eat a lot, and rest a lot."

—**Hugh Jackman**

"Broadway has been very good to me. But then, I've been very good to Broadway."

—**Ethel Merman**

"The only stuff I don't like are Broadway musicals. I hate them. I don't even like to talk about it. I can't bear musicals."

—**Laurie Anderson**

# NY's Finest (Parks)

*Even the most urban New Yorkers need a bit of greenery every now and then.*

## Riverbank State Park

The amazing thing about this park is its location: on top of a building in Manhattan. And not just any building; it's on the roof of a working wastewater treatment plant, covered with tons of trucked-in soil. Situated along the Hudson River, the 28-acre park features a grassy area for picnics, several trees, an Olympic-size swimming pool, a skating rink (roller-skating in the summer and ice-skating in the winter), an 800-seat theater, tennis and basketball courts, a restaurant, and a pedestrian esplanade that allows walkers views of Manhattan and the New Jersey Palisades across the river.

## Letchworth State Park

Located 60 miles southeast of Buffalo in Livingston County, this 14,350-acre park is home to "the Grand Canyon of the East," Letchworth Gorge. It's a 22-mile section of the Genesee River that contains three deep, stunning gorges, the middle of which, the Great Bend Gorge, plunges 550 feet. The river forms three sizable waterfalls within the park, and dozens more flow into it from the cliffs above—several of which are more

*Middle Falls at Letchworth State Park*

than 500 feet tall themselves. The park was named after William Pryor Letchworth, a Buffalo businessman and philanthropist who donated the land to the state as a public park in 1906.

*Riverbank State Park sits atop a wastewater treatment plant.*

## Goosepond Mountain Park

Near the village of Chester in New York State's Lower Hudson Valley is this park for people who like a rustic experience: It's almost completely undeveloped. There are no toilets, no running water—it's even hard to find a parking space. Most of the park is pure woods and wetlands, and there are many miles of trails, which include wooden walkways over the wetlands, offering especially good viewing of a wide variety of waterfowl. Goosepond also has some interesting history: A rocky outcrop in the park hides a small rock shelter that, according to legend, was used as a hideout by the notorious Claudius Smith, leader of a group of Loyalist guerrillas known as the "Cowboys," who terrorized the region during the Revolutionary War.

## Jones Beach State Park

This park takes up almost all of Jones Beach Island, one of the long, narrow barrier islands off Long Island. Its most popular feature: more than six miles of sandy beach along the Atlantic Ocean. Jones Beach is the most-visited beach on the East Coast—with some 6 million people passing through every year—so don't go there for a quiet getaway. The park also has two huge old bathhouses, built in 1920s Art Deco style, a 231-foot water tower, and a two-mile-long stretch of boardwalk. All of the buildings were designed by the park's chief founder, Robert Moses.

## Adirondack Park

The largest state-protected park in the contiguous United States, Adirondack Park covers an astounding 9,375 square miles—an area roughly the size of Vermont. It's home to the Adirondack Mountains, more than 3,000 lakes (including Lake Placid, the site of two Winter Olympics), more than 2,000 miles of hiking trails, thousands of miles of rivers and streams, and a huge variety of mammals, including black bears, moose, coyotes, lynx, otters, beavers, and porcupines.

- Adirondack Park is larger than Yellowstone and Yosemite National Parks…combined.

- It's considered a unique example of publicly and privately owned parkland. About 46 percent of the park—2.7 million acres—is a state-owned forest preserve. That land is protected by the New York State constitution as "forever wild." The rest of the park is privately owned, although most of it is forest and sparsely developed farmland.

- There are 103 towns and villages within the park's boundaries, and about 137,000 people live there year-round.

- The Adirondack Mountains have 46 peaks more than 4,000 feet high, including Mt. Marcy, the state's highest, at 5,344 feet.

- There are no official entrances to Adirondack Park, and there is no entrance fee. Just drive, bike, walk—or canoe—right in.

# Roadside Attractions

*Next time you're on a road trip and need a break, consider one of these New York pit stops.*

- **The Upside-Down Traffic Light** (a.k.a. Green on Top): Syracuse

- **World's Largest Kaleidoscope:** Mount Tremper

- **The 300-Pound Concrete Foot:** Manhattan

- **World's Largest Dead Shark:** Vanderbilt Museum, Centerport, Long Island

- **The 50-Foot-Tall Teepee:** Cherry Valley

- **Carousel Capital of the World:** Binghamton

- **The Hello Kitty Fountain:** Manhattan

*Rick Krane restores the largest taxidermy specimen in the world, the dead whale shark at the Vanderbilt Museum.*

# New York Food from Q to Z

*Our smorgasbord of New York's favorite edibles and grazing grounds continues. (A to P appears on page 28).*

**Queens:** The city's most culturally diverse borough, famous for its variety of restaurants. Among the cuisine you'll find: Greek, Moroccan, Middle Eastern, Egyptian, Afghan, Czech, Spanish, French, Italian, Romanian, Indian, Pakistani, Filipino, Mexican, Brazilian, Thai, Peruvian, Chilean, Colombian, Argentine, Ecuadoran, Salvadoran, Cuban, Uruguayan, Japanese, Chinese, and Korean.

**Reuben Sandwich:** This grilled sandwich of corned beef, Swiss cheese, sauerkraut, and Russian dressing on rye has murky origins. New York deli owner Arnold Reuben either invented it or let it be named for him, but food historians continue to argue the point. (A few claim it was invented in Nebraska, but no New Yorker believes that for a minute.)

**Snapple:** Born in Greenwich Village in 1972, when Hyman Golden, Leonard Marsh, and Arnold Greenburg (owner of a health-food store on St. Mark's Place) started making and selling fruit drinks. By

*A typical Reuben sandwich is packed with corned beef.*

1989, their small company, Unadulterated Food Products (later the Snapple Beverage Corporation) made 53 different flavors.

**Thousand Island Dressing:** Invented in the Thousand Islands–Seaway resort region of upstate New York, probably around 1910, by the wife of a popular fishing guide. She gave her recipe to actress May Irwin, who coined the dressing's name. May passed the recipe to George Boldt, proprietor of the Waldorf-Astoria, and George gave it to his maitre d'—who promptly put it on the hotel's menu.

**Ukrainian Food in Brighton Beach:** Brighton Beach is where the great Russian food is, and serious foodies are happy to make the pilgrimage out there to eat dumplings, kebabs, kasha, pickled vegetables, and a *lot* more (quantity is part of the experience). BYOB (vodka, of course), but the custom is to keep the bottle out of sight under the table.

**Vietnamese Bánh Mì:** These sandwiches have taken

New York by storm, especially in Queens, Brooklyn, and Manhattan. Think French/Vietnamese fusion: a Vietnamese baguette (made with wheat and rice flours) stuffed with ham, pork, pâtè, pickled vegetables, and sometimes basil, cilantro, mayo, cucumbers, or bean sprouts.

**Whitefish, Smoked:** Like chopped liver, smoked fish isn't a New York invention, but it's been raised to a high art at Zabar's, Barney Greengrass, and Murray's Sturgeon on the Upper West Side, Russ & Daughters on the Lower East Side, and other "appetizing shops." (An "appetizing shop" is a store that specializes in things you can eat on bagels.)

**XO Sauce:** Chinese sauce made with dried shrimp, dried fish, and dried scallops cooked with red chili peppers, onion, garlic, and oil; typically served with Cantonese meals and dim sum in restaurants. Invented in Hong Kong in the 1980s, but it's now a New York City staple.

**Yonah Schimmel's Knishes:** In 1910 Yonah Schimmel, a rabbi from Romania, opened his bakery on East Houston Street, where he made only kasha, potato, and fruit-and-cheese knishes (filled dumplings).

*Tofu in XO sauce*

The shop is still there, and it hasn't changed much—except now you can get a veggie egg roll, potato kugel, or even a chocolate knish.

**Zito's Bread:** This one got away, and New Yorkers still miss it. Zito's coal oven–baked white, semolina, and whole wheat were the best breads you could get until well into the 1960s. A family-run fixture on Bleecker Street since 1924, it closed in 2004.

*Zito's bread was beloved by New Yorkers until the store closed in 2004.*

# City Hodgepodge

- New York County (Manhattan) is the most densely populated county in the United States. Kings County (Brooklyn) is #2.
- Some inmate dormitories at Rikers Island are located inside former Staten Island Ferry boats docked at the prison.
- Manhattan lies along the same latitude as the temperate Mediterranean region of Europe, so when the early Dutch settlers arrived in New York, they were shocked that the winters were so cold and snowy.
- Central Park is larger than the kingdom of Monaco.
- There is no Main Street in Manhattan, but each of the other boroughs has one.
- Trees required to print the Sunday *New York Times*: 75,000.

*A boy plays at the Brooklyn Children's Museum.*

- Only school in the world to offer a college degree in Cosmetics and Fragrance Marketing: the Fashion Institute of Technology in Manhattan.
- About 47 percent of New York City residents older than five speak a language other than English at home.
- Alexander Hamilton founded the *New York Post* in Manhattan in 1801. It's the longest continuously running daily paper in the United States.
- More than 3 million people have been buried in Calvary Cemetery in Queens, making it the "most populous" cemetery in the United States.
- About 40,000 location shoots for movies, TV shows, and commercials take place in New York City every year.
- The Brooklyn Children's Museum, which opened in 1899, was the first museum in the world created specifically for kids.

# Mob, Inc.

*In the 1920s and '30s, mob bosses ruled the mean streets of New York City.*

## La Cosa Nostra

Throughout the 1920s, New York was terrorized by criminals. Gangs threatened business owners, extorted money, corrupted labor unions, and formed gambling, prostitution, and drug rings. Some of the most successful criminal organizations were controlled by Italian American immigrants who, in 1931, stopped battling each other, joined forces, and created a criminal syndicate known as La Cosa Nostra, or the American Mafia.

La Cosa Nostra ran its illegal activities like a corporation: The newly allied gang lords served on an executive board called the Commission, which gave orders to the rest of the mob. Charles "Lucky" Luciano, the architect of La Cosa Nostra, was the first head of the Commission. Like all good businessmen, Luciano ran his corporation to create big profits. And like all good criminals, he used violence to intimidate people and keep his enemies in check.

## Mobilizing the Troops

To help provide the kind of "muscle" La Cosa Nostra needed, Luciano enlisted two gangster pals—Meyer Lansky and Benjamin "Bugsy" Siegel. Lansky was known for his business brains and organizational skills, and Siegel was an accomplished hit man. Even though they were not Italians (they were from Jewish crime networks), Luciano brought Lansky and Siegel into La Cosa Nostra because they had done "enforcement" for other gang lords—dealing out beatings and killing people who ran afoul of organized crime. Together, Luciano, Lansky, and Siegel formed a Brooklyn-based gang of contract killers whose job was to commit murders for La Cosa Nostra.

Luciano also brought in Louis Buchalter, a gangster who had taken control of New York's garment industry unions and then used that influence to extort factory owners by threatening strikes and walkouts. On Luciano's watch, Buchalter became the boss of the contract killers. Albert Anastasia, who controlled the city's waterfront, was put in charge of day-to-day operations. Buchalter was said to be so cold that his eyes "were like blocks of ice," and Anastasia was a brutal bully known as the "Lord High Executioner." Under this grim pair, the Brooklyn hit squad became so efficient at killing victims for the Mafia that the public began calling it "Murder Inc."

*Bugsy Siegel*

*Charles "Lucky" Luciano enjoys a drink at the Excelsior Hotel in Rome.*

## Murder's Heyday

Like traveling salesmen, the members of Murder Inc. often took their deadly services on the road. In 1939, when the New York bosses worried that union mobster Harry "Big Greenie" Greenberg was no longer loyal and might turn informant, a Murder Inc. assassin was called in to kill him. The hit man chased Greenberg from Montreal to Los Angeles. There, the hired killer stalked and assassinated Greenberg, the first organized-crime murder in L.A.

Buchalter paid his hit men about $12,000 a year (nearly $200,000 in today's dollars), plus bonuses. The mob expected professionalism, and Murder Inc. operatives prided themselves on their skill and efficiency. They could kill with a knife, an ice pick, a garrote, a machine gun, or their bare hands, depending on what would get the job done quickly and not get them caught.

## Hard to Catch

The U.S. government estimated that Murder Inc. killed about 1,000 people across the country, and the hit men were hard to catch. When the law did track one down, La Cosa Nostra guaranteed him the best defense possible. The mob also tended to kill witnesses and tamper with juries, so hit men often walked.

One other problem was that police and lawyers didn't even know how far La Cosa Nostra's reach was. In 1940, when Burton

*Residents pack a street in the Brownsville section of Brooklyn in the early 1900s. Murder Inc. based its operations in that neighborhood.*

## Business at Midnight

The headquarters for Murder Inc. was in the Brownsville section of Brooklyn, in a 24-hour candy store called Midnight Rose, on Saratoga Avenue. The location was convenient for the hit men, who came mainly from the Jewish, Irish, and Italian gangs in the neighborhoods of Brownsville, Ocean Hill, and East New York. They gathered at the store for meetings and used pay phones out back to get their assignments from the Commission. Orders to kill usually came directly from Buchalter himself.

The victims, whom the assassins called "bums," were usually other gang members. Many were suspected police informants or had committed some act of disloyalty, such as pocketing gang profits that were supposed to be paid to the bosses. Police officers and other lawmen were rarely targets because La Cosa Nostra wanted to avoid retribution from the authorities.

*Meyer Lansky was a high-ranking member of La Cosa Nostra.*

Turkus became Brooklyn's assistant district attorney, he inherited a collection of unsolved murders. At the time, no one knew they were all connected to Murder Inc. As Turkus later wrote: "If anyone had suggested that the 200 or so unsolved murders plaguing us…could be laid to the same group of killers, we would have laughed at them."

## Bringing Down Murder Inc.

In the end, a simple case of loyalty finally unraveled Murder Inc.'s reign of terror. In 1940 small-time hoodlum Harry Rudolph saw a 19-year-old friend get shot in the back by members of Murder Inc., so he wrote to the district attorney's office, volunteering information. When detectives followed up on Rudolph's tip, they were able to arrest three members of Murder Inc., including Abe "Kid Twist" Reles—a man so high in the gang hierarchy that he knew all the inside details.

To save himself from the electric chair, Reles spilled all his secrets. After he'd outlined the workings of Murder Inc., 85 unsolved murders in New York were solved and six members of the gang were convicted of homicide and executed. Even the powerful Louis Buchalter went to his death in Sing Sing's electric chair. As Murder Inc. weakened, more of its members scrambled to avoid the death penalty by turning inform-ant. Within just a few years, the deadliest gang in America was disbanded. And as for the leaders:

- Lucky Luciano ran La Cosa Nostra until 1935, when he was finally sent to jail for running a prostitution ring. (Many of his associates insisted that Luciano was framed, arguing that he was too high up in the organization to deal directly with prostitutes.) During World War II, his mob contacts spied for the U.S.

government, and to reward him, he was freed and deported to Italy in 1946. He died there of a heart attack in 1962.

- Bugsy Siegel moved to California in 1935, where he continued working for the mob. In 1946 he built the Flamingo, a luxury hotel and casino in Las Vegas. After construction problems delayed the opening of the casino, his investors thought

*Louis Buchalter was sentenced to death in 1941.*

Siegel was skimming profits. They had him gunned down in 1947.

- Meyer Lansky became Luciano's financial advisor and ran things when Luciano went to prison. The government prosecuted Lansky for tax evasion in the early 1970s, but the mobster fled to Israel. He tried to become a citizen there, but was returned to the United States. He was acquitted at trial and lived quietly, dying of lung cancer in 1983. Because Lansky had been expert at hiding money in Swiss banks, some said he went to his death leaving $400 million in secret accounts...even though his family said he was broke.

# Trash in a Box

**Artist:** Justin Gignac
**Medium:** Authentic New York City garbage
**The art:** Around 2003, when Gignac was working as an intern at MTV, he got into a debate with a coworker who claimed that a product's packaging was unimportant to its success; what really mattered was the product inside. Gignac dis-agreed—packaging, he said, was everything. To test that theory, he went around New York City collecting trash (ticket stubs, plastic forks, scraps of subway maps, and so on), and then artfully arranged the pieces inside small, sleek plastic cubes. He called the creations "Garbage of

*Gignac's work*

New York City" and started selling them on the street for $10 each. To make the garbage "exclusive," Gignac signed each cube and attached a sticker with the date the garbage was collected. It worked. He eventually raised the prices...to $50 (for regular trash) and $100 (for "limited edition" trash—garbage from opening day at Yankee Stadium, or a Times Square New Year's Eve celebration). By 2008 he'd proven his point by selling more than 1,000 cubes. What kind of trash worked best? Gignac says, "I only pick up dry trash. Wet trash would rot in the cubes and, besides, I'm a bit squeamish."

# On Broadway

*You can't have a Broadway play without a Broadway theater. Here are some behind-the-scenes facts about the big-money theaters that make it all happen.*

- A "Broadway play" does not necessarily mean that a show is being produced at a theater on Broadway itself. Instead, it indicates the size of the theater. Broadway venues are the ones with the most seats: 500 or more. (Off-Broadway theaters have 100 to 499 seats; off-off-Broadways have fewer than 100.)

- All of the Broadway theaters happen to be in New York's main theater district in Times Square, through which Broadway Avenue runs. One exception: the Vivian Beaumont Theater, which is at Lincoln Center.

- Only five theaters have a Broadway address. The rest are in the West 40s and 50s.

- Currently, there are 40 Broadway theaters. Most are large—30 of them seat more than 1,000.

- Largest Broadway theater: the Gershwin, with 1,935 seats. Smallest: the Helen Hayes Theater, with 597 seats.

- Of the 40 theaters, 17 are owned by the Shubert Organization, which owns more than 50 theaters in New York City... including the Shubert Theater.

- Total number of seats in all the Broadway theaters put together: 49,670. (Total number of seats in the new Yankee Stadium: 50,287.)

- Oldest operating Broadway theaters: the Lyceum and the New Amsterdam, both built in 1903. In 1974 the Lyceum became the first Broadway theater to be named a historical landmark. The New Amsterdam is the earliest example of the Art Nouveau architectural style in New York City.

- Latest Broadway theater to close: Henry Miller's Theatre, in 2004, although a new theater was built on the site, and renamed the Stephen Sondheim in 2010.

- The famous Studio 54 disco was converted into a theater in 1998. The first production on Studio 54's stage: *Cabaret.*

- Like sports stadiums, many Broadway theaters have changed their names to reflect corporate sponsorship. One current example: the American Airlines Theatre.

- Other theaters are named after theatrical icons, such as musical composer Richard Rodgers, playwright Eugene O'Neill, actress Ethel Barrymore, and longtime *New York Times* theater critic Brooks Atkinson.

- The New Amsterdam is corporate-owned by Disney, for its stage-musical adaptations, but the company opted not to rename it because of the building's historical importance.

*The Broadway Theater District entices visitors from all over the world.*

123

# New York Inventors

*If it weren't for the state of New York, the world would be without many important products.*

## George Eastman

A high-school dropout from Waterville, George Eastman changed the way we see the world when he invented rolled photography film in 1885. The creation did away with the delicate glass plates and messy gelatin emulsions used in photography at the time and made it easier for everyone to document the world around them. Eastman continued to take photography mainstream over the next decade with the invention of the handheld, push-button camera.

*After George Eastman (left) invented photography film, he worked with Thomas Edison (right) to make motion pictures possible.*

## Linus Yale Sr.

Linus Yale Sr. of Salisbury helped Americans feel more secure in 1848 when he invented the pin-tumbler lock, a cylindrical mechanism that employs rods of various lengths to prevent a lock from being opened without the appropriate key. The design was later modified in 1875 by his son, Linus Yale Jr., and remains popular today.

*Linus Yale Jr. (above) used an ancient Egyptian wooden lock with pins, like this one (right), as a model when he invented his pin-tumbler lock.*

## Willis Haviland Carrier

Anyone who has ever used an air conditioner to cool off on a hot day has Willis Haviland Carrier to thank. This Angola engineer outsmarted Mother Nature in 1902 when he created the first air-conditioning unit to control the heat and humidity levels in a Brooklyn printing plant. Carrier continued to refine his invention, and by 1915 he was selling his "Apparatus for Treating Air" to grateful clients all around the world.

*Jonas Salk appeared on the cover of* Time *on March 19, 1954.*

## Jonas Salk

In 1948 New York City native Jonas Salk was the head of the Virus Research Lab at the University of Pittsburgh when he first began work on a way to eradicate the dreaded polio virus. Salk's experiments proved to be successful, and by 1952 he had created a safe and effective polio vaccine that he tested on his wife and three sons. Nationwide testing began two years later, and by 1955 America's "Polio Panic" had become a thing of the past. Salk's breakthrough made him a national hero and led to the creation of the Salk Institute, a leading independent scientific research center located in San Diego, California.

## George Crum

The head chef at a resort in Saratoga Springs, George Crum unwittingly made history in 1853 when a notoriously hard-to-please patron sent back a plate of French fries, complaining they were too thick. Fed up with the patron's frequent complaints, Crum tossed several thin slices of potatoes

*George Crum and his sister-in-law, "Aunt Kate" Weeks, in 1853*

into a pan, fried them to a crisp, and covered them with a generous helping of salt. To his surprise, the patron loved them, and Crum's "potato chips" soon became a staple on his menu. By the 20th century, potato chips had made their way into millions of American homes.

*Joseph C. Gayetty*

## Joseph C. Gayetty

In 1857 New York City inventor Joseph C. Gayetty brought some much-needed relief to Americans when he created the world's first commercial toilet paper. Marketed as a means to cure sores and prevent hemorrhoids, Gayetty's Medicated Paper contained 500 individual sheets moistened with soothing aloe; each package sold for 50¢.

*The Greatest Necessity of the Age!*
## GAYETTY'S Medicated Paper, FOR THE WATER-CLOSET.

*Elvis Costello performs "Radio Radio."*

### Pierre Lorillard IV

*Pierre Lorillard IV*

This wealthy tobacco magnate found himself on everyone's best-dressed list in October 1886, when he wore a tailless black jacket and matching black tie to a formal ball at the Tuxedo Club in Tuxedo Park, New York. He may have heard about King Edward VIII of England wearing a similar outfit—some say as early as 1875. Regardless, after the Tuxedo Club's ball, news soon spread, and it wasn't long before socialites were sporting "tuxedos" at formal functions all around the country.

# Forgive and Forget

In the 1970s, Elvis Costello was hugely famous as a British punk and new wave rocker, so of course *Saturday Night Live* wanted him to be a musical guest. On December 17, 1977, Costello got the gig...by accident. The Sex Pistols, who were supposed to perform that night, couldn't get their passports in order, so they couldn't travel. *SNL* producer Lorne Michaels called on Costello, who agreed to do the show.

Michaels had some conditions, though. Mainly he insisted that Costello not perform the song "Radio Radio," which criticized the media's power to decide what the public would and would not hear, a form of censorship...just what Michaels was trying to do. Surprisingly, Costello agreed and showed up to perform as scheduled.

When Costello and his band, the Attractions, stepped onstage, they launched into another hit, "Less Than Zero," but suddenly, Costello signaled for the band to stop, said there was no reason to play that song, and then proceeded to play "Radio Radio." Lorne Michaels was furious. Not only had Costello violated his directive, but the stop and start made the entire show run long. Michaels banned Costello from future appearances on *SNL*.

It took 12 years for Michaels to get over the over the incident, but on September 26, 1999, Costello made his second *Saturday Night Live* appearance... and played "Radio Radio."

# The Miracle Mets

*Only 25 percent of New Yorkers admit to being Mets fans. But over the years, the Amazins have managed some amazing comebacks.*

- The Mets played their inaugural season in 1962 and didn't get a win until the 10th game. They ultimately lost 120, the most losses in one year in modern MLB history. But by 1969 the team was playing its best season yet, winning 100 games, sweeping the Atlanta Braves to win the National League pennant, and finally beating the Baltimore Orioles in five games to win the World

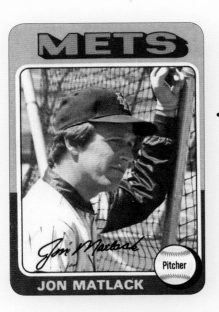

Series, the first expansion team ever to take the title. The season earned them the nickname "the Miracle Mets."

- During a May 1973 game at Shea Stadium, Atlanta Brave Marty Perez cracked a line drive right into the forehead of Mets pitcher Jon Matlack. The ball hit Matlack so hard that it fractured his skull and then bounced off one of the dugouts. Many

Mets players and fans thought Matlack's career was over, but he returned to the mound just 11 days later to pitch a win in Pittsburgh.

- By the late 1970s, the Mets had fallen into the "losers" category once again, and in 1979, they posted just 63 wins... and 99 losses. Shea Stadium sat nearly empty throughout the season, earning it the nickname "Grant's Tomb." But the team rallied during the 1980s, signing stars like Darryl Strawberry and Gary Carter. By 1986 they'd rebounded once again to appear opposite the Boston Red Sox in the World Series. By game six, all appeared to be lost—the Red Sox were up 3–2, and one of the scoreboards even flashed a congratulatory message to the Boston team. But the Mets went on to stage one of the most

*Far left: Citi Field, home of the Mets*
*Left: Darryl Strawberry bats in 1983.*

impressive comebacks in baseball history. Thanks to a lot of timely hitting—and an infamous error from Boston first baseman Bill Buckner, who let a slow ball roll through his legs—the Mets went on to win game six, and then game seven, to take their second World Series title.

- On April 17, 2010, the Mets beat the St. Louis Cardinals 2–1 in a 20-inning game that lasted for seven hours. It was the first time in MLB history that neither team scored in the first 18 innings.

*Below: Ryan Ludwick of the St. Louis Cardinals is tagged out by Rod Barajas of the New York Mets on April 18, 2010.*

*Gary Carter bats against the Pittsburgh Pirates in 1989.*

*The first* New Yorker, *February 21, 1925*

# Low Turnover

The *New Yorker* has no masthead (the list that most magazines include up front, calling out the names of all the people who work there), a tradition since its early days. So it's hard to track the comings and goings of the staff. Maybe it's also because there is so little turn-over: In its more than 85 years in print, the *New Yorker* has had only five chief editors. Cofounder Harold Ross edited

the magazine for its first 26 years. He was a whirlwind of energy, working at least 10 hours a day. Sometimes he was pessimistic, grumbling, and prone to temper tantrums, but he was still considered a brilliant editor—idiosyncratic and well-liked. His death from cancer in December 1951 at the age of 59 was a terrible blow to the staff and writers. But by then, the *New Yorker* was so well established that its

managing editor, William Shawn, could step right into the editor-in-chief's job in January 1952. Shawn edited the magazine until 1987—he was followed by Robert Gottlieb (until 1992), Tina Brown (to 1998), and the current editor, David Remnick.

# Murder, He Wrote

*How did New York City, a famous cigar girl, and Edgar Allan Poe combine to create one of the world's first murder mystery stories? Read on.*

## Prologue

Anyone who enjoys murder mysteries owes a debt of gratitude to Edgar Allan Poe. Before there was a Sherlock Holmes or a Nancy Drew, before the word "detective" was even in common usage, Poe created the character of C. Auguste Dupin, an eccentric Parisian genius who solved murder cases that baffled the city's police force. Dupin first appeared in April 1841 in a short story called "The Murders in the Rue Morgue" and reappeared in two more stories after that. To create his detective stories, Poe did plenty of research on real crimes, including one of his century's most notorious murder mysteries.

*In this illustration from "The Purloined Letter," Dupin switches letters as the minister looks out at the street.*

*Edgar Allan Poe*

## Chapter One: The Body

On July 28, 1841, the body of 21-year-old Mary Cecilia Rogers was found floating in the Hudson River near Hoboken, New Jersey. The discovery was shocking, not just because the body was battered beyond recognition (she could be identified only by her clothing and a birthmark on her arm), but because Rogers was famous in New York City. One of America's first celebrities, she was nicknamed the "beautiful cigar girl."

Until shortly before her death, Rogers had worked at a huge tobacco and cigar shop on Broadway. She had an unusual job: enticing men into the shop. According to legend, she was so beautiful that men would come inside just to see her…and wouldn't leave without buying tobacco. Some of those admirers even published poems in local papers, singing of her charms. One besotted "poet" wrote, "She's picked for her beauty from many a belle / And placed near the window Havanas to sell." Other patrons were more talented, including New York City newspaper reporters and a writer named Edgar Allan Poe.

## Chapter Two: The Disappearance

By July 1841, Rogers had quit her job at the tobacco shop to help her mother run a boardinghouse on Nassau Street. She had plenty of admirers there, too, including a sailor named William Kiekuck, clerk Alfred Crommelin, and the dashingly handsome (but hard-drinking) Daniel Payne. To her mother's dismay, Rogers chose Payne and accepted his marriage proposal, though there were rumors later that the young woman was planning to leave him.

On Sunday, July 25, Rogers told her fiancé that she was going to visit her aunt, who lived uptown. She never made it. When she hadn't returned home the next morning, Payne took out a missing persons ad in the *New York Sun*. Reporters jumped on the story—search teams formed and started combing the city. But Rogers was nowhere to be found…until Wednesday, when her body was pulled from the river. The coroner found strangulation marks on Rogers's neck, and part of her dress had been torn off and tied around her mouth and neck with a sailor's slipknot. Another piece of her dress was missing, and the coroner speculated that it had been used to drag the body to the river. He also noted that Rogers was not pregnant, she had been severely beaten and sexually assaulted, and her body still showed signs of rigor mortis (when a corpse's limbs go stiff). He concluded that she'd been murdered on Sunday night, just after she left home, and that she may have been killed by more than one assailant, perhaps one of the gangs that plagued New York City's streets at the time.

## Chapter Three: The Investigation

The discovery of the beautiful cigar girl's body launched an intensive inquiry to find out who had killed her. Some people thought she'd drowned accidentally, but that didn't explain her injuries. One witness claimed to have spotted her on Sunday on the Hoboken Ferry with a "dark-complected man." Daniel Payne and the other men she knew from the boardinghouse came under suspicion immediately; newspapers even published libelous stories accusing them of her murder. Payne had to bring witness affidavits to several city newspaper offices to get them to stop calling for his arrest.

About three weeks after Rogers disappeared, a woman named Frederica Loss, who ran a tavern in Hoboken near the spot where Rogers's body was found, came forward and produced some stained, mildewed pieces of clothing that she said her sons had found nearby.

The items looked like things Rogers had owned—one handkerchief was even mono-grammed with the initials "MR." But no one knew for sure that the items had belonged to Mary Rogers, and there were rumors that the belongings had been planted to lure gawkers. Loss's tavern had been doing a brisk business serving tourists who came to visit the site of Rogers's demise.

## Chapter Four: The Revelation

Despite having several leads, police couldn't find Rogers's killer. Every suspect they questioned (including her fiancé, Daniel Payne) had an alibi. But events began to take a strange turn. In October 1841, a few

*An 1841 illustration shows Mary Rogers in the river.*

months after Rogers's death, Payne walked to the thicket near Hoboken where Rogers's clothes had been found. There, he penned a vague note about his "misspent life" and drank a fatal overdose of laudanum, a liquid form of opium.

Then, in the fall of 1842, one of Frederica Loss's sons accidentally shot her. On her deathbed, a delirious Loss confessed that on that fateful Sunday, Mary Rogers and a doctor had rented a room in the tavern. Rogers was pregnant, Loss said, and she died in the rented room from complications after the doctor performed an abortion.

That story appeared in all of New York City's major newspapers and churned up reader interest again. Police found nothing to corroborate the confession, but the case was back in the spotlight. Questions abounded: A botched abortion contradicted the coroner's report that Rogers had died of strangulation. Had the coroner been lying? Or had the mysterious doctor tried to cover the whole thing up by beating Rogers's body, simulating a strangulation, and dumping her in the river? Could the wounds from the abortion have looked to the coroner like sexual assault? Maybe Mary Rogers was planning to leave Daniel Payne after all, and when he found out about that and the abortion, he killed her in a fit of rage. Or was Frederica Loss simply a delusional, dying woman still trying to drum up business for her tavern? No one knew, and no one ever figured it out. To this day, Mary Rogers's murder remains unsolved.

## Chapter Five: The Detective Story

In 1841 Edgar Allan Poe wasn't yet the legend he is today, but he was an up-and-coming writer. He'd held jobs at various literary magazines and had published several short stories, including "The Murders in the Rue Morgue," starring that early fictional detective C. Auguste Dupin. Poe had always been attracted to stories of supernatural melancholy and horror, and Mary Rogers's murder caught his attention. He decided to try to solve the case in fictional form, and to write a compelling story in the process. The result was "The Mystery of Marie Rogêt," a three-part

serial that appeared in a magazine called *Snowden's Ladies' Companion* in late 1842 and early 1843. Poe wrote later, "Under the pretense of showing how Dupin...unraveled the mystery of Marie's assassination, I, in fact, enter into a very rigorous analysis of the real tragedy in New York."

Poe's story went like this: The body of a young woman named Marie Rogêt was pulled out of the Seine River in Paris. The perfume-shop worker had been beaten and died as the result of some kind of "accident." Part of her dress had been removed and tied in a

sailor's knot, which was used to drag the body to the river.

In the story, Dupin essentially "solved" the crime by implying that Rogêt had been killed by a "naval officer with [a] dark complexion." But Poe never named names. "The Mystery of Marie Rogêt" was a hit for Poe, and so was the final Dupin story, "The Purloined Letter," published in 1845. It also spawned an entirely new fictional genre: the detective novel, which turned crime-solving into literature.

*"The Mystery of Marie Rogêt" appeared in this issue of the* Ladies' Companion, *published in November 1842.*

# Café des Artistes, Manhattan

The Café des Artistes opened in 1917 on the lobby floor of the Hotel des Artistes (a building of artists' studios on West 67th Street) for the purpose of providing meals for the hotel's residents. The much-coveted studios had plenty of windows, but no kitchens, so the artists brought their own ingredients and the café's chefs prepared their meals. The café evolved into a beautiful restaurant with murals of nymphs (painted by resident artist Howard Chandler Christy in 1934), lush flower arrangements, and soft lighting. It became a destination for performers, musicians, and artists—a clientele that increased after Lincoln

Center opened in the early 1960s. Famed restaurateur George Lang bought the Café des Artistes in 1975. Lang had managed the Four Seasons restaurant from 1967 to 1969, and then pioneered the field of international restaurant consulting, working with hotel corporations like Marriott and Sheraton. If anyone should have been able to keep the Café des Artistes going, it was Lang—and for many years it was a great success under his leadership. But by 2009, business was down, union-related costs were soaring, Lang was 85, and the curtain finally came down on one of New York's most romantic dining spots.

# For Sale: A Bridge in Brooklyn

*"If you believe that, I have a bridge to sell you" has insulted gullible people since the 1800s. It comes from the days when con artists actually "sold" the Brooklyn Bridge to tourists and immigrants, most of whom expected to make a fortune on tolls from travelers between Brooklyn and Manhattan. (They didn't.)*

**Swindler:** Reed C. Waddell

**Sale Date:** 1880s through mid-1890s

**Price:** Unknown

**Details:** Born in Springfield, Illinois, Waddell moved to New York in 1880 and started conning people right away. He offered the Brooklyn Bridge to gullible folks and pioneered a "gold-brick scandal" in which he passed off lead bricks plated with gold as solid-gold ones. Over several years, he made about $250,000.

**Closing Costs:** In 1895 Waddell was shot and killed by fellow criminal Tom O'Brien, with whom he'd been arguing over shares of a heist.

**Swindler:** Brothers Charles and Fred Gondorf

**Sale Date:** Early 1900s

**Price:** $200 to $1,000 (Once, the Gondorfs sold *half* the bridge for $250 to someone who couldn't afford the whole thing.)

**Details:** The brothers were professional con men who had a surefire way to avoid detection: As soon as police officers crossed the bridge one way on their beat, the Gondorfs whipped out "Bridge for Sale" signs, chose their marks, and collected cash.

*This 1920s photo of the Brooklyn Bridge captured a well-dressed man (second from left) whom some historians think is swindler George C. Parker.*

They knew roughly the length of a beat path (though it varied, depending on how much crime was going on at a given time) and always broke down the enterprise before the cops returned.

**Closing Costs:** The men also ran a horse-racing scam. In 1915 Charlie was caught and imprisoned for that. Fred soon joined his brother after he was arrested for wire fraud. Neither was ever arrested for the Brooklyn Bridge con. In 1973, long after they'd died, the brothers gained fame on the big screen: They were the inspiration for the grifters Johnny Hooker (Robert Redford) and Henry Gondorf (Paul Newman) in the movie *The Sting*.

**Swindler:** George C. Parker

**Sale Date:** Twice a week for several years during the 1920s

**Price:** From $50 to $50,000, with payment plans available

**Details:** Parker convinced his marks that he was a legitimate businessman by presenting them with "official" ownership documents that listed him as the property holder for the Brooklyn Bridge. The documents were forged, of course, but they fooled many people. Sometimes it took months for the duped buyers to realize the bridge wasn't theirs—and often they figured out they'd been conned only after they tried to set up toll booths and were stopped by police. Parker went on to "sell" Madison Square Garden, General Ulysses S. Grant's tomb, and even the Statue of Liberty.

**Closing Costs:** Parker was caught when he scammed three Texans who had him arrested. Facing his third fraud conviction, he got a life sentence. He died in Sing Sing in 1936.

*Robert Redford (left) and Paul Newman play con men in* The Sting.

# Cheers for Beers

*Move over, Milwaukee. Step aside, St. Louis. We're paying tribute to another American brewing capital: Brooklyn.*

## Brooklyn Born and Brewed

Between the 1840s and Prohibition in 1920, there were at least 35—some say as many as 50—breweries in Brooklyn. In Williamsburg and Bushwick alone, a dozen of them dotted a 12-block section that became known as Brewer's Row (Scholes and Meserole Streets from Bushwick Avenue to Lorimer Street). Heavy, British-style ales came first. Later, German immigrants introduced their own style of Bavarian lager. But for all the popularity of Brooklyn beers, even big brand names like Rheingold and Schaefer, they never could compete with national brands, so they remained regional favorites.

## My Beer Is Rheingold

Of all the beers brewed in Brooklyn, Rheingold was the one people knew best, thanks to a ubiquitous ad slogan, "My beer is Rheingold, the dry beer." By the 1950s, the phrase had been turned into a jingle that played all over New York City's TV and radio stations. The brand was introduced by the Leibmann family—father Samuel and sons Joseph, Charles, and Henry—who came to Brooklyn from Bavaria around 1850. Soon after, they opened their first brewery on Meserole Street, and then moved to expanded facilities at Forrest and Bremen Streets in Bushwick 1855.

Expert marketers, Rheingold hired a list of celebrity endorsers that would make

*A beer ad features the 1949 Miss Rheingold.*

today's promoters foam with envy: Groucho Marx, John Wayne, Marlene Dietrich, Gene Kelly, Dean Martin, Ella Fitzgerald, Cab Calloway, Carmen Miranda, and many more. In 1956, when *The Nat King Cole Show*—the first successful TV variety program to feature a black host—had trouble finding sponsors, Rheingold signed on. When the New York Mets set out to fill the baseball gap created after the turncoat Dodgers and Giants fled to California, Rheingold was among the team's charter sponsors. The Miss Rheingold competition, held annually from 1941 to 1964, generated millions of votes from the public, occasionally outpacing national elections. The beauty contest also attracted a number of young women who became Hollywood stars, including Hope Lange and Tippi Hedren. (Neither won the title.) Competition was tough: In the 1948 Miss Rheingold contest, Grace Kelly didn't even make the final cut.

## "When You're Having More Than One"

The Bavarian-style lager beer introduced by the F. & M. Schaefer brewing company in the 1840s was a revelation to New York beer drinkers. "Its merits were many," wrote the *New York Times* in 1885, "including vivacity, brilliancy, and coolness, without the 'gummy,' soporific, and changeable characteristics of ale."

Light, thirst-quenching Schaefer quickly became, as its slogan said, "the one beer to have when you're having more than one." And beer drinkers did indeed have more than one. In 1885 Schaefer was brewing 150,000 barrels a year, in 1938 the company passed the million-barrel mark, and in 1944 it produced two million barrels a year. Not bad for a business started by two kids from Germany.

Frederick and Maximilian Schaefer immigrated to New York in the 1830s. After working at a brewery in Manhattan for a couple of years, they bought it in 1842. Frederick was 25 years old; Maximilian was 23. They built new facilities on Seventh Avenue and 17th Street, and then moved uptown to Fourth Avenue

*A 1955 ad for Schaefer beer and the Brooklyn Dodgers*

*Fidelio brewed and delivered McSorley's ales until the 1940s.*

(now Park Avenue) and 51st Street, where the company headquarters remained for 67 years before it relocated to Kent Avenue in Brooklyn. (St. Bartholomew's Church and the Waldorf-Astoria were built on Park Avenue sites once owned by Schaefer.)

As Schaefer expanded, its production branched out to Pennsylvania and Maryland. But by the 1970s, sales had

dropped and the big Brooklyn plant was no longer a jewel in the company crown. Schaefer announced it would close the plant in 1976, just a week after Rheingold revealed it was closing its own Brooklyn facility. Thus, the reign of the big-time Brooklyn breweries came to an end.

## Honorable Mention: McSorley's

This one's not in Brooklyn, but old-time New York drinking establishments don't get more old-timey than McSorley's Old Ale House at 15 East Seventh Street in Manhattan. The place has been going strong since John McSorley opened the doors in 1854. Abraham Lincoln drank there. Woody Guthrie sang there. E. E. Cummings wrote a poem about it. But for the bar's first 116 years, if you wanted that old-time experience and you happened to be a woman, you were out of luck. McSorley's didn't have a lot of rules, but "no ladies" was one of them. Even when the bar was owned by a woman, which it was from 1939 to 1974, women didn't drink there. The owner, Dorothy O'Connell Kirwan, who inherited the place from her father, only came in on Sundays after the bar was closed. Finally, in 1970, a judge's ruling forced McSorley's to let women in. (It took

another 16 years for a women's restroom to be installed.)

The other rule at McSorley's—one that remains essentially unbroken—is that the bar serves only ale. No wine, no cosmopolitans or appletinis, no light beer or lager. Just McSorley's ale—in light and dark varieties, served two at a time in half-pint glasses. Fidelio Brewery on First Avenue and 29th Street brewed the first ales for McSorley's, but today they're brewed by Pabst. And while you can buy McSorley's in bottles now, nothing compares to hoisting a cold one at the ale house itself.

## Some Big Apple Moviemaking Facts

- In 2006 the city scored 34,718 on-location shooting days, up from 21,286 in 1996.
- In 2007, 88 percent of New Yorkers said they had seen filming taking place in the city—and 95 percent of Manhattan residents had.
- Los Angeles's share of total production dropped from 54 to 48 percent in 2008, but New York's climbed from 12 to 15 percent.
- New York City offers a free "production assistant training program" for low-income or unemployed residents as part of its Made in NY campaign to bring moviemaking to the city.

# Changed by Fire

*One of the greatest tragedies in New York's history led to some of today's most important safety regulations. If you've ever wondered why your office is always holding fire drills, read on.*

*Firemen fight the Triangle Shirtwaist Factory fire.*

## Unlucky #9

On March 25, 1911, the Saturday shift was just ending at the Triangle Shirtwaist Factory, which occupied the eighth, ninth, and tenth floors of the Asch Building near Washington Square. Shirtwaists—light cotton women's blouses—were all the rage at the time, and the factory floor was lined with bins full of cotton waste scraps. Fabric was draped over sewing tables, and tissue-paper patterns hung from clothes-lines. Workers—mostly young Jewish women who'd recently immigrated—were collecting their pay and getting ready to go home. But what they didn't know was that a small fire had started in one of the waste bins on the eighth floor. The fire quickly spread to fabric and paper nearby, and within minutes, the whole eighth floor was engulfed in flames.

Most of the workers on the eighth floor escaped. A bookkeeper called up to the offices on the tenth floor and warned the owners. They immediately fled, along with almost everyone on the tenth floor. But no one was able to get through to the workers on the ninth floor. As the fire spread below them, the ninth-floor workers were trapped. One survivor said, "All of a sudden, the fire was all around."

## No Way Out

At the time, garment factories like the Triangle Shirtwaist one dotted Manhattan, and safety regulations were well-established. But many factories ignored them, and Triangle, owned by Max Blanck and Isaac Harris, was among the worst violators. When the Asch Building was built in 1901, an automatic sprinkler system would have cost $5,000, so the owners decided to leave it out. The building's fire hose wasn't maintained—a manager tried to use it to put out the flames, but found that the hose had rotted and the valve was rusted shut. Some workers knew there was a fire escape, but those who climbed out onto it found that the drop ladder, which was supposed to extend down to the alley, had never been installed. The weight of so many workers on the narrow fire escape tore it from the building, plunging two dozen people to their deaths.

Worst of all, only one of the doors to the two stairwells could be opened—the other was kept locked to prevent employee theft. The stairwell that was open was quickly blocked by fire when a barrel of machine oil (that had been stored in the stairwell) exploded. The fire spread so fast that many workers never even had time to leave their sewing machines. And those who tried to escape were faced with an impossible choice: Helpless onlookers watched in horror as dozens of people jumped to their deaths to avoid the flames.

## NYU to the Rescue!

From a neighboring building, law students at New York University could see hundreds of people, mostly from the tenth floor, on the roof of the Asch Building. The students

*Max Blanck (left) and Isaac Harris owned the factory.*

sprang into action, laying ladders across the gap between roofs and rescuing about 150 people. Firemen arrived at the scene within minutes and quenched the blaze a half hour after it started, but it was too late—146 people were dead.

The Asch Building, which had been certified fireproof, had lived up to its billing—it didn't burn, but *everything* inside did.

## Changes

After the Triangle fire, the city sent inspectors out to other factories. Most were found to be violating city safety codes. Within a few years, New York passed comprehensive building codes and fire safety laws—at the time, the strictest in the nation, all as a direct result of the Triangle fire. The tragedy was a turning point for the safety of American workers in other industries, too. It served as a catalyst to the growing union movement, which gave workers more leverage to force factory owners to improve working conditions, and New York State reorganized its Department of Labor so it could more effectively regulate factories. Other states adopted the changes too, and eventually, the reaction to this fire—which killed so many low-income workers—even laid the groundwork for the creation of a federal minimum wage.

The owners of the Triangle Shirtwaist Factory, meanwhile, were charged with manslaughter for locking the stairwell…but were acquitted. The insurance claims they filed for the fire made them a tidy profit of $400 for every victim. ($75 of that was eventually awarded to each victim's family, after a civil suit.) Two years after the Triangle fire, one of the owners was arrested for locking an exit door in another factory he owned. This time he was found guilty…and fined $20.

The Asch Building still stands. Renovated and renamed the Brown Building, it's now part of the NYU science department.

*Above: The commemoration of the fire's 100th anniversary drew thousands of people, many waving shirtwaists with the victims' names.*
*Below: The scorched ninth floor of the factory was where most of the workers died.*

# Reclaiming Central Park

*From above, Central Park looks like a big green rug lying in the middle of Manhattan Island. But from the ground, it's a lot more complicated, with 843 acres of careful landscaping...and 150 years of history.*

## Birth of a Park

Until the mid-1800s, New York City had no great public park. People got away from the noise and chaos of city life by visiting the few quiet open spaces they could find. (Cemeteries were among the most popular spots.) On hot summer days, wealthy people could go to the country, but the poor were trapped in the sweltering city. Influential New Yorkers began to push for a centrally located park that would offer meadows, lakes, fountains, and woodlands for everyone to enjoy. Popular 19th-century journalist William Cullen Bryant wrote, "If the public authorities who expend so much of our money in laying out the city would do what is in their power, they might give our vast population an extensive pleasure ground for shade and recreation... which we might reach without going out of town."

In 1853 the state legislature agreed to let New York City acquire 700-plus acres (it was later expanded) in the center of Manhattan, an area that had been home to a cluster of small villages and settlements built on rocky, swampy soil. (Part of the reason the land was considered good for a park was that it wasn't suited for commercial use.) The Central Park Commission held a landscape design competition, and landscapers Frederick Law Olmsted and Calvert Vaux won. Their plan: to shape the natural scenery around a minimum amount of architecture. In 1873 Central Park was completed.

*Robert Moses*

*New York's skyscraper-fringed Central Park serves as a refuge from city life.*

## Share and Share Alike

Unfortunately, the new park was still far away from where most poor people lived, and train fare was expensive. Workweeks were long—six days a week, usually—so they could get to the park only on Sundays. Two small but important things finally made the park more attractive to working-class people: regular Saturday afternoon concerts were moved to Sundays, and the first Central Park playground was built in 1926. Soon the park was in constant use for strolling, picnics, sports, and other recreations—but with so many people using it, the park soon fell into disrepair.

## The Good Moses Years

Robert Moses began his political life as an idealist. In 1920 his progressive ideas for getting rid of corruption in Albany brought him to the attention of Governor Al Smith and put him on the road to power

Skating in Central Park, *painted by Agnes Tait in 1934, highlights some of New Yorkers' favorite winter activities.*

in the state. Though Moses was never elected to office, he worked hard behind the scenes. And when President Franklin Delano Roosevelt's New Deal offered the city millions of dollars in the early 1930s, Moses was ready with plans to spend much of it on public works. Building parks, housing, highways, bridges, and tunnels in New York City and New York State became his life's work.

In 1934 he was appointed the New York City Parks Commissioner. By that time, Central Park was full of dead trees, untended lawns, broken benches, and litter. Moses changed all that: The park's purpose, in his view, was not to be a natural landscape (as Olmsted and Vaux had envisioned), but to be a playground for New Yorkers. He built ball fields; handball, croquet, and shuffleboard courts; a revamped zoo; bridle paths; and more playgrounds.

Moses also paid attention to park maintenance. His crews repaired bridges and walls, replanted lawns and flowers, and replaced trees. But he also implemented new rules for park behavior—for example, no bathing suits, no halter tops, and shorts had to come at least to mid-thigh. Moses liked things to be done his way, and the more power he had, the more autocratic he became.

*Families stroll through Central Park in this 1934 painting by Carl Gustaf Nelson.*

## The Bad Moses Years

One day in 1956, after Robert Moses had reigned over the park system for two decades, a group of mothers discovered that their children's playground on the west side of Central Park was about to be destroyed to build a parking lot for the ritzy Tavern on the Green restaurant. The mothers staged a protest that was soon dubbed the "Battle of Central Park." First, they wrote a petition against the bulldozing. When that had no effect, they held a rally in front of Tavern on the Green. That got Moses's attention—he promised a prompt reply, but instead sent bulldozers onto the playground a few days later. The mothers and their children stood in front of the bulldozers, and they halted the project. The same thing happened the next day and the next, but then Moses had his crew sneak into the park in the middle of the night, put up a fence around the play area, and start bulldozing trees. The press

*Belvedere Castle is home to the summer Shakespeare plays in Central Park.*

was all over the story, and a judge ordered a cease-fire. Moses backed off. In one day, the mayor received 4,000 letters of protest against his actions. It ultimately took three months and a court battle, but the playground was finally restored. The incident badly damaged Moses's reputation. And that was just the beginning. In the late 1950s, Joseph Papp—the producer who later established the Public Theater—had been delighting audiences with free presentations of Shakespeare in the park. Funding the shows was always a problem, and Papp continued his efforts to raise the money from foundations—but he wanted Moses's Parks Commission to help fund the program. Moses, however, staunchly opposed the city subsidizing free theater in the park (or anywhere else). He also didn't like Papp and considered him to be something of a bully. Why? Those Shakespeare plays were performed near Belvedere Lake, and according to Moses, Papp "presumed the area was his."

In 1959 Moses demanded that Papp charge an admission fee to cover the cost of "grass erosion." Papp, who, by most reports, was as rigid as Moses, refused and took Moses to court. After a storm of negative publicity and a bitter legal battle, Moses agreed to withdraw his demand and to build Papp a proper amphitheater in the park. But Moses never recovered from the scandal. In May 1960, he resigned as commissioner.

## Fun Park in Fun City

John Lindsay became mayor in 1966 and promptly dubbed New York "Fun City." To make Fun City even more fun, he appointed Thomas P. F. Hoving as parks commissioner. Although Hoving was commissioner for just a year, he managed in that short time to stage dozens of "Hoving Happenings"—band concerts, Halloween events, kite-flying, a "Central Park A-Go-Go" dance concert, and other

spectacles that drew enormous crowds into Central Park. He even closed the park to traffic on Sundays—and when visitors loved that, he closed it to traffic on Saturdays, too. His successor, August Heckscher, kept the Central Park events coming.

But from the late 1960s through the early 1970s—while Commissioners Hoving and Heckscher were sponsoring happenings, performances, and parties—the crime rate in Central Park was on the rise. As more and more people used the park, more of them became victims of crime. In addition, upkeep had become a concern again. From 1969 until 1977, New York City suffered from the same recession that plagued the rest of the country. The city's financial woes got worse and worse, and if there wasn't enough money for police and schools, how could there be enough for parks? Central Park once again became a shambles: Gardens were neglected, meadows wore down to dusty ground, benches fell apart, statues deteriorated, and bridges were defaced by graffiti. By the end of the 1970s, concerned citizens felt it was time to step in.

## Publically Private and Privately Public

In 1980 the Central Park Conservancy was formed, a unique partnership between the Parks Department and a group of civic leaders who saw that Central Park could not be restored to its original beauty and purpose without help from the private sector. Under a special agreement, the Parks Department retained control of park policy, while the Conservancy took responsibility for the park's day-to-day maintenance and operation—and for raising the money to do it. Today, 75 percent of the park's $58 million annual budget is controlled by the Conservancy, and 80 percent of the park staff is employed by it. The city pays for lighting, maintenance of park roads, 20 percent of the park staff, and the Central Park Police Precinct.

Since the Conservancy began, it has raised more than $390 million in private money that, added to the $110 million contributed by the city, has made it possible to restore the Great Lawn, Bethesda Terrace, and the Harlem Meer, and to create Strawberry Fields, named in honor of John Lennon. Conservancy crews tend 130 acres of woodland, 250 acres of lawn, and 150 acres of lakes and streams; maintain 9,000 benches, 26 ball fields, and 21 playgrounds; and preserve 36 bridges. They remove graffiti within 24 hours of finding it and dispose of 5 million pounds of trash each year. The park is now a beautiful and safe haven for New Yorkers and tourists. How safe? In the early 1980s, there were 1,000 crimes reported per year in Central Park; in 2013, there were only 103.

*The lower passage of Bethesda Terrace is one of the most famous spots in Central Park.*

# "Start Spreadin' the News"

Frank Sinatra's 1980 version of "New York, New York" may be the best-known song about the Big Apple, but Sinatra wasn't the first to sing it. Liza Minnelli sang "New York, New York" in Martin Scorsese's 1977 film of the same title. The song was written for the film by Fred Ebb and composed by John Candor, and in the years since, it's been covered by countless other artists in various genres, including Queen, Sammy Davis Jr., Phish, Michael Bublé, and Devin Townsend, who did a heavy-metal version for a compilation album called *SIN-atra*.

The song, which captures the pride and spirit of the "city that never sleeps," is played regularly during the Macy's Thanksgiving Day Parade, in Times Square on New Year's Day just after the ball drops and, until recently, at the end of every home game in Yankee Stadium— Sinatra's version when the Yanks won; Minnelli's version when they lost.

*Robert DeNiro and Liza Minnelli appear in* New York, New York.

# The Last List

*The world is full of firsts, but from the city that has everything, we bring you a list of lasts.*

*Gimbel's is seen on the left in this 1958 postcard of Herald Square.*

## Last Time the Macy's Thanksgiving Day Parade Went Down Broadway

November 27, 2008. In 2009 the city changed the route to accommodate more viewers, eliminating the run down Broadway.

## Last Time There Was a Shutout at Ebbets Field

September 24, 1957, when lefty Danny McDevitt and the Brooklyn Dodgers beat the Pittsburgh Pirates 2–0. That game also happened to be the last played at Ebbets Field.

## Last Time Streetcars Ran in Brooklyn

October 31, 1956. They were pushed out by buses and personal automobiles.

*The restored Brooklyn streetcar No. 1053 was built in 1947.*

## Last Time You Could Shop at Gimbel's

September 26, 1986. The department store, much loved and co-featured in the movie *Miracle on 34th Street*, closed September 27.

## Last Time Eddie Cantor Floated Down Broadway

November 21, 1940, when his likeness was made into a balloon for the Macy's Thanksgiving Day Parade. Technically, this was also the *only* time the Eddie Cantor balloon was featured in the parade. Kids found his image "scary." (The Three Stooges also once enjoyed their own balloon images.)

## Last Time You Could Smoke in NYC's Bars and Restaurants

2003, when the city council passed a resolution banning smoking inside public places. In 2011 the city council passed another law banning smoking at the city's parks and beaches. The punishment for defying the ban: a "quality of life" summons that'll cost you $50.

*Kermit, Uncle Sam, and other floats are ready to go during the 2008 Macy's Thanksgiving Day Parade.*

## Last Time You Could Dance at the Original Studio 54

Early in the morning of February 4, 1980. The club closed later that day when managers Steve Rubell and Ian Schrager were fined and sent to prison for 3½ years on charges of conspiracy and tax evasion. The club reopened briefly several times over the years, but never achieved the original's notoriety or fame.

*Partygoers dance the night away inside the original Studio 54.*

*Judy Garland (right) plays the Palace Theatre in 1967 with her children Lorna and Joey Luft.*

## Last Time Judy Garland Played the Big Apple

November 17, 1968, when she sang "Over the Rainbow" at a Lincoln Center tribute to songwriter Harold Arlen.

## Last Time New York Was *Not* America's Largest City

1809. The following year, New York City surpassed Philadelphia in population to reach #1, a title it hasn't relinquished since.

## Last Time You Could Be Part of the Studio Audience for the *Ed Sullivan Show*

February 7, 1971. The program was canceled shortly afterward.

## Last Time You Could Check into St. Vincent's Hospital in Manhattan

2010. In April the board voted to close the hospital due to Chapter 11 bankruptcy.

## Last Time You Could Ride in a Checker Cab in the City

July 26, 1999. The last vehicle was about 17 years old at its retirement.

## Last Time You Could Dump Your Trash at Fresh Kills Landfill on Staten Island

March 22, 2001, although the dump was temporarily reopened for burial of 9/11 attack debris. The 2,200-acre area is now being developed into a park.

## Last Time Mastodons Roamed New York City

Around 11,000 years ago, according to scientists who studied a mastodon jawbone found by construction workers near Broadway and Dyckman Streets back in 1925.

*Mastodon*

*Fresh Kills in all its putrid glory.*

# Picture Credits

*Multiple credits per page are listed in a clockwise sequence.*

*Front cover:* Steve Kelley aka mudpig | Getty Images; Dana Rothstein | Dreamstime.com; Chromakey | Shutterstock; Marie C Fields | Shutterstock; Easyshoot | Dreamstime.com; Thinkstock/iStock, Romanovskyy
*Back cover:* Dennis K.Johnson | Getty Images

• 2 Brett Critchley | Dreamstime.com • 6 Ron Sumners | Dreamstime.com • 7 Barna Tanko | Dreamstime.com; Og-vision | Dreamstime.com • 8 Volodymyrkrasyuk | Dreamstime.com; PD; PD • 10 NBC | NBCU Photo Bank | Getty Images; Collection of the Smithsonian National Museum of African American History and Culture, 2008.16.1–.3; Melissa Mergner | Jazz Times • 11 Alan Fisher | Library of Congress; Photoquest | Dreamstime.com • 12 Steve Kelley | Getty Images • 13 Marcorubino | Dreamstime.com • 14 PD; PD | Leopoldo Galuzzo • 15 CNN | nypost.com/2010/02/25/network-falls-for-140-year-old-hot-dog-hoax/; AP | AAP |Frankie Ziths; David Clegg | Shutterstock • 16 christopherreach.com; PD | Christian Schussele • 17 CC |Axel Drainvillea; PD • 18 Mikhail Kusayev | Dreamstime.com; Spencer Platt | Getty Images • 19 pennilesstraveler.com/2013/08/14/unique-new-york-5-quirky-things-to-do-in-manhattan/; PD; Mario Burger | Burger International Photography; Peter Kramer | NBCNewswire | Getty Images • 20 PD; Eastmanphoto | Dreamstime.com • 21 Dmitry Maslov | Dreamstime.com; Christopher Forsyth; TVGN | CBS | moviestillsdb.com • 22 Richard Perry |The New York Times | Redux; Gabriele Stabile | The New York Times | Redux; Bialasiewicz | Dreamstime.com; Iev Radin | Shutterstock • 23 PD; Littleny | Dreamstime

• 24 PD; PD | George Catlin • 25 Tim Martin | Dreamstime.com; PD | Library of Congress • 26 Paramount | Getty Images; Alison Grippo | Dreamstime.com • 27 Breakers | Dreamstime.com • 28 Mo Tipton | The Mouse Market; Tatyana Chernyak | Dreamstime.com • 29 Julie Feinstein | Dreamstime.com; www.hellmanns.com; Natursports | Dreamstime.com; • 30 Sanja Grujic | Dreamstime.com; www.youtube.com/watch?v=yZSFt2xIr3w; MorganOliver | Dreamstime.com • 31 /www.city-data.com/forum/new-york-city/1870934-vintage-new-york-city-signage.html; Brett Critchley | Dreamstime.com • 32 Touchstone Pictures | Buena Vista Pictures | MovieStillsDB; Centropolis Entertainment | Twentieth Century Fox | MovieStillsDB; Goldcrest Films | Avco Embassy Pictures | MovieStillsDB • 33 Centropolis Entertainment | Lionsgate | 20th Century Fox | MovieStillsDB; Sweetshutter | flickr.com; Black Rhino Delphi Productions | Columbia Pictures | MovieStillsDB • 34 Carrienelson1 | Dreamstime.com; Carrienelson1 | Dreamstime.com; Sbukley | Dreamstime.com; www.aceshowbiz.com/events/Ojani%20Noa/wenn267184.html; Dimitri Halkidis | WENN; Bryan Busovicki | Dreamstime.com • 35 Pernacca Sudhakaran | United Nations Photo; CC |Beyond My Ken • 36 PD | Library of Congress; Sean Pavone | Dreamstime.com • 37 The LIFE Picture Collection | Getty Images • 38 CC | L. Adam; roadsideamerica.com/story/16703 • 39 Zhukovsky | Dreamstime.com; Bob Davidson | Flickr • 40 Julie Larsen Maher | AP | AAP | Wildlife Conservation Society ; BettyB | Flickr • 41 Julie Larsen Maher | Wildlife Conservation Society • 42 Jurijcorr | Dreamstime.com; PD • 43 Joel Gordon | Joel Gordon Photography; Misty Pfeil | Dreamstime.com; Howard Simmons |NY Daily

News | Getty Images • 44 PD • 45 PD; Dell Publishing • 46 PD | Fred Palumbo | JoeJohnson2; Thierry Boccon-Gibod | Gamma-Rapho | Getty Images • 47 Andrew Bernstein | Getty Images; Matthew X. Kierman | New York Big Apple Images • 48 Brett Critchley | Dreamstime.com • 49 PD | John Sloan; Featureflash | Dreamstime.com • 50 PD; HBO | MovieStillsDB; www.pinterest.com/pin/49328558388673985/ • 51 www.queensfarm.org; ~Nicholas | Flickr; CC | Gertrude Vanderbilt Whitney • 52 barbettarestaurant.com; CC | Thomas doerfer—Eigenes Werk • 53 Barry Winkler | Getty Images; Time & Life Pictures | Getty Images; CC | Alan Light; Imagecollect | Dreamstime.com; Biscuits & Bath | biscuitsandbath.com • 54 RKO Radio Pictures | MovieStillsDB; RSO Records | Paramount Pictures | MovieStillsDB; Jurrow-Shepherd | Paramount Pictures | MovieStillsDB • 55 Marvel Entertainment | MovieStillsDB; CC | Gage Skidmore • 56 Lembi Buchanan | Dreamstime.com; Ben Hider | Getty Images • 57 Shannon McGee | flickr • 58 PD; Steve Lovegrove | Dreamstime.com • 59 John Skelson | Flickr; PD | Columbia Pictures • 60 Littleny | Dreamstime.com; CC | Beyond My Ken; Pixdesign123 | Dreamstime.com • 61 Ron Galella | WireImage | Getty Images; Typhoonski | Dreamstime.com • 62 CC | Beyond My Ken; Zhukovsky | Dreamstime.com • 63 Los Angeles Times Archive | UCLA; Warner Bros. | Getty Images | Dreamstime.com • 64 Sheena Chi | Flickr ; CC | Anthony22; Frank Bender | U.S. General Services Administration • 65 Homeriscool | Dreamstime.com; Paul Prescott | Dreamstime.com • 66 PD; Willeecole | Dreamstime.com • 67 Rebekah Burgess | Dreamstime.com; PD | Helayne Seidman

142

• 68 Aaron Landry | Flickr • 69 Eddie Toro | Dreamstime.com • 70 Young Money, Cash Money, Republic; PD; CC | Sfoskett • 71 PD; Marc A. Hermann | Polaris; unknown • 72 George Karger | The LIFE Images Collection | Getty Images; Mychal Watts |WireImage |Getty Images • 73 Ebet Roberts | Redferns |Getty Images; Aija Lehtonen | Dreamstime.com • 74 PD | Chester Harding; PD • 75 PD • 76 Russ Glasson | Landov Media | Barcroft Media • 77 Sharon Cornet | www.sunstar-solutions.com/rachel2004.htm; Doug and Carla Balduini |www.pinebushufo.com/pinebushpage35.htm • 78 CC | Allen Warren; Timothy A. ClaryI |AFP |Getty Images • 79 PD | Elliott Landy |Redferns |Getty Images; Gamma-Keystone |Getty Images • 80 unknown; Tom Hauck | Getty Images; D. Carr and H. Craighead | Cornell • 81 PD; Kidwiler Collection | Diamond Images |Getty Images • 82 David Hernandez | Dreamstime.com; Bigapplestock | Dreamstime.com; blueclue | iStock • 83 NYU; www.nydiamonddistrict.com/NY-Diamond-District-47th-Street-Photo-Gallery.html • 84 Mark Rucker | Transcendental Graphics | Getty Images • 85 Jerry Cooke | Sports Illustrated | Getty Images; Waite Hoty Collection | Cincinnati Museum Center | Getty Images • 86 Joe Traver | Getty Images • 87 PD | Library of Congress; PD | Edward Harrison May • 88 CC | Alexisrael; CC | Ira Goldstein; CC | Beyond My Ken; Lombardi's |openplac.es/trips/lombardi-s-in-new-york-ny |www.firstpizza.com/links.html; • 89 Union College | plus.google.com; jewishcurrents.org/wp-content/uploads/2011/09/Kunstler.jpg; PD • 90 John Anderson | Dreamstime.com; PD | Elon Howard • 91 Lincoln Karim| palemale.com • 92 David Gahr | Getty Images; Littleny | Dreamstime.com • 93 CC | Historystuff 2 • 94 Michael Putland | Getty Images; Michael Ochs Archives | Getty Images • 95 Slim Aarons | Getty Images • 96 PD; PD; Jeff Stein | Dreamstime.com • 97 PD; Alexandre Fagundes De Fagundes | Dreamstime • 98 Lars Christensen | Dreamstime.com, Dennis Albert Richardson | Shutterstock, L. Adam; Mattias Klum | National Geographic Creative

• 99 The New York Botanical Garden • 100 Underwood Archives | Getty Images; Archive Holdings Inc. | Getty Images • 101 www.nycedc.com/project/la-marqueta • 102 storingupforwinter.blogspot.com.au/2007/10/mario-batali-youre-my-hero-im-gonna-eat.html; www.whyleaveastoria.com/profiles/blogs/astorias-king-of-falafel-wins; Adeliepenguin | Dreamstime.com • 103 www.nycgo.com/slideshows/vendy-award-winners-2013/3; Breakers | Dreamstime.com • 104 Chester Higgins Jr. | The New York Times | Redux images; PD; PD • 105 Brendan McDermid | Reuters | Picture Media; Carmen Taylor | WireImage | Getty Images; PD | Skybunny • 106 Dan Cronin | NY Daily News Archive | Getty Images; Marianne Campolongo | Dreamstime.com • 107 John P. Kelly | Getty Images • 108 PD; PD; Eugene L. Armbruster | The New York Historical Society | Getty Images • 109 Matt Lambros | Matt Lambros Photography; PD • 110 Time Inc.; PD | Fred Palumbo | Library of Congress; PD | U.S. Navy; Omnibus | Wikimedia • 111 Linda Naklicki | WNYC Archive Collections; CC | Jim Henderson • 112 Sbukley | Dreamstime.com • 113 Steve Lovegrove | Dreamstime.com • 114 Thomas Monaster | NY Daily News | Getty Images; CBS Photo Archive | Getty Images • 115 Andrew Toth | FilmMagic | Getty Images; Scott Levy | NHLI | Getty Images • 116 PD | Jim Henderson; Gary Koutsoubis | Getty Images • 117 CC |Doug Ker; Rick Krane | Anglers Artistry, Hinsdale • 118 Ppy2010ha | Dreamstime • 119 ErwinPurnomaSid | Dreamstime; Shiningcolors | Dreamstime; Westvillagebob | Flickr • 120 PD | Remo Nassi; New York World-Telegram and the Sun Newspaper Photograph Collection | Library of Congress; PD | Library of Congress • 121 Irving Underhill | Brooklyn Museum | Brooklyn Public Library, Brooklyn Collection; PD | Al Ravenna | Library of Congress • 122 PD | Edward Lynch | Library of Congress; Justin Gignac • 123 Luciano Mortula | Dreamstime • 124 Time Inc.; PD; PD; AP | AAP • 125 PD; PD; NBC | NBCU Photo Bank | Getty Images • Harold Seton | NY Daily News Archive | Getty Images; PD • 126 PD; Ron

Vesely | MLB Photos | Getty Images; Gerald Mothes | Dreamstime.com; PD • 127 Rick Stewart | Getty Images; The New Yorker | Condé Nast; Dilip Vishwanat | Getty Images • 128 PD • 129 PD • 130 PD; CC | WSTM Team Boerum 0072 • 131 PD; Universal Pictures | MovieStillsDB • 132 PD; CC | wallyg • 133 PD • 134 PD •135 CC | Triangle33; PD • 136 www.gothamgazette.com/index.php/development/3402-jane-jacobs-robert-moses-and-city-planning-today; Songquan Deng | Dreamstime.com • 137 Carl Gustav Nelson | Smithsonian American Art Museum, DC | Art Resource, NY; Agnes Tait | Smithsonian American Art Museum, DC | Art Resource, NY • 138 Songquan Deng | Dreamstime.com • 139 Rudi1976 | Dreamstime.com; United Artists |MovieStillsDB • 140 PD; Rob Corbett | Dreamstime.com; PD • 141 Waring Abbott | Getty Images; Waring Abbott | Getty Images; PD; Digital Light Source | UIG | Getty Images; Ron Galella | WireImage | Getty Images

# The Last Page

FELLOW BATHROOM READERS:
The fight for good bathroom reading should never be taken loosely—we must do our duty and sit firmly for what we believe in, even while the rest of the world is taking potshots at us.

We'll be brief. Now that we've proven we're not simply a flush-in-the-pan, we invite you to take the plunge: Sit Down and Be Counted! Log on to *www.bathroomreader.com* and earn a permanent spot on the BRI honor roll!

If you like reading our books...
## VISIT THE BRI'S WEBSITE!
*www.bathroomreader.com*

- Visit "The Throne Room"—a great place to read!
- Receive our irregular newsletters via email.
- Order additional *Bathroom Readers*.
- Read our blog.

*Go with the Flow...*

Well, we're out of space, and when you've gotta go, you've gotta go. Tanks for all your support. Hope to hear from you soon. Meanwhile, remember...

*Keep on flushin'!*